HOW GOOD
IS
YOUR ENGLISH?

In the same series

THE RIGHT WAY TO IMPROVE YOUR ENGLISH

HOW GOOD IS YOUR ENGLISH?

TEST YOURSELF AND SEE!

by

CEDRIC ASTLE, B.A.(Hons.)

PAPERFRONTS

ELLIOT RIGHT WAY BOOKS
KINGSWOOD, SURREY, U.K.

Made and printed in Great Britain by
Hartnolls Ltd., Bodmin, Cornwall.

CONTENTS

PART ONE

PART TWO

HOW GOOD *IS* YOUR ENGLISH?

Do you read, speak and write it with ease and confidence?

Or do you confess to moments of embarrassment when faced with its exasperating uncertainties? –

Those SPELLING snags, for instance:

Is it *seize or sieze*? – *medicine* or *medecine*? – *dessicated* or *desiccated*?

The PRONUNCIATION dilemma:

Do you *pass* or *pahss*? Is it *vahz*, *vawz* or *vayz*? And how do you pronounce: *chiropodist*, *formidable*, *harem*, *precedence*, *schedule*?

The PUNCTUATION explosion:

Do you believe in *womens*' rights – or in *women's*? Does *snack bar* need a hyphen? Is she *your's* sincerely – or *yours*?

Problems of USAGE:

Should I *try and* or *try to* do it? Was it *due* to the strike, or *owing* to it? Is this the *most unkindest* cut of all?

Do you find equally tantalising problems when you turn from Language to Literature? –

Which of the Brontë sisters wrote *Wuthering Heights*?

Was it Sheridan or Goldsmith who wrote *She Stoops to Conquer*?

Lord Jim and *Lucky Jim* – Who wrote which? (Kingsley Amis or Joseph Conrad?)

Which poet wrote: "Water, water everywhere . . .?"

And which wrote: "Let us have wine and women,
mirth and laughter,
Sermons and soda-water the day after"?

If this random spot-check has revealed disquieting gaps in your general knowledge of the subject, here is a book to help fill the gaps and remove that feeling of inadequacy.

HOW GOOD IS YOUR ENGLISH is a multi-purpose book, comprising proficiency tests (with answers and definitions) and word lists.

To well-informed and confident readers, the book is offered as a "Top of the Form" or "University Challenge" test of attainment. They may even be tempted to work systematically through the questions in Part One without reference to the answers.

Students, it is hoped, will regard it as a source book, as a companion, not an alternative, to the teaching of English through free expression and creative writing. In English examinations at all levels, candidates are still required to express themselves in "good English" (with all the expression implies) and to have some knowledge of the literature in which the best may be found.

Part One
QUESTIONS

I

HOW DID IT START ?

Every student of English should know something of the history and development of the language. Were you aware, for instance, that nearly sixty per cent of the words in an English dictionary are of Romance origin (i.e. derived from Latin roots)? The influence of Greek is also strong; and through centuries of war, travel, commerce, colonisation, scientific invention and discovery, the vocabulary has been enriched by borrowings from many languages.

At the same time, it is still true to say that English is basically a Teutonic language. The grammar is essentially Teutonic, as are the words most commonly used by speakers and writers.

The following questions are based upon a study of *origins:*

1. Has your home town an Old English name? Or could the name be of Latin, or Celtic, or Danish origin? Which of the four elements can you recognise in the italicised parts of these place names?

<table>
<tr><td>Aberfan</td><td>Avonmouth</td><td>Caithness</td><td>Leicester</td></tr>
<tr><td>Exeter</td><td>Tamworth</td><td>Boscombe</td><td>Stratford</td></tr>
<tr><td>Margate</td><td>Llangollen</td><td>Cromford</td><td>Sidholme</td></tr>
<tr><td>Lowestoft</td><td>Stockport</td><td>Inverary</td><td>Rotherham</td></tr>
<tr><td>Fosbridge</td><td>Sheffield</td><td>Stanton</td><td>Lincoln</td></tr>
</table>

Give, if you can, the meaning of each italicised portion.

2. Four Latin 'invasions' of the language, each with its crop of new terms, may be represented by these significant dates:

A.D. 410 597 1066 1453

Can you say what happened in each case?

3. Here are five other memorable dates in the history of the English language:

A.D. 1258 1348 1362 1477 1611

Why are they important? Select your answers from the following table of events, which are *not* given in chronological order:

(*a*) Printing introduced into England by Caxton.
(*b*) Authorised Version of the Bible issued.
(*c*) English used in Law Courts.
(*d*) Parliament proclaimed in English.
(*e*) English first taught in schools.

4. The words in each of the following groups have a common Latin root. Can you find the meaning of the root by studying the word family derived from it? –

(*a*) altar, altitude, alto (*altus*)
(*b*) domain, domineer, dominion (*dominus*)
(*c*) confide, fidelity, infidel (*fides*)
(*d*) liberal, libertine, liberty (*liber*)
(*e*) manacle, manual, manuscript (*manus*)

5. Now do the same with these groups:

(*a*) portal, portcullis, portico (*porta*)
(*b*) consecrate, sacrament, sacrilege (*sacer*)
(*c*) adumbrate, umbrage, umbrella (*umbra*)
(*d*) abundant, inundate, undulate (*unda*)
(*e*) deviate, obviate, viaduct (*via*)

6. Can you give two common English words derived from each of these Latin roots? Say what the root word means in each case:

centum	*dictum*	*erratum*	*flexum*	*gradus*
cantum	*corpus*	*annus*	*homo*	*lectum*

7. Which of these words are of Latin origin, and which are derived from the Greek?

capital	acrobát	alibi	astrology	autograph
benefit	bible	epigram	brevity	doctor

8. Many English word-families are of Greek origin. (e.g. amphi*bio*us, *bio*graphy and *bio*logy have the common Greek root, *bios*.) Can you deduce the meaning of the Greek root in each of the following groups?

(*a*) anther, anthology, polyanthus (*anthos*)
(*b*) dermatology, epidermis, hypodermic (*derma*)
(*c*) dialogue, epilogue, logic (*logos*)
(*d*) anachronism, chronicle, synchronize (*khronos*)
(*e*) microbe, microphone, microscope (*mikros*)

9. In group (*a*) below, you will find ten common Greek roots from which English word-families have been derived. Find two examples of each in group (*b*), then by studying the meanings of these words try to give the meaning of each Greek word:

(*a*)

lithos	*pathos*	*kuklos*	*oxus*	*isos*
klimax	*phone*	*theos*	*demos*	*metron*

(*b*)

bicycle oxygen monolith atheist pathetic
symmetry isosceles cyclone theology
gramophone barometer lithograph anticlimax
paroxysm isobar demagogue euphony
sympathy democracy climacteric

10. Can you find *doublets* (i.e. words derived from the same roots but different in form and meaning) for the following words?

(*Example:* fragile – *frail*)

antic amiable gentle royal secure

11. Can you name the language from which each of the following words was imported into English? You will find the answer in group (*b*):

(*a*) *WORD*

chess banana giraffe souvenir typhoon
waltz alcohol oasis balcony marmalade

(*b*) *LANGUAGE*

Spanish African Chinese German French
Persian Arabic Italian Egyptian Portuguese

12. In these examples of borrowings from various languages, word and language are wrongly paired. Can you put them right?

moccasin (Mexican) stucco (Dutch)
bungalow (Hebrew) garage (North American)
chocolate (Italian) sabbath (Hindustani)
paper (French) yacht (Danish)
husband (African) chimpanzee (Egypt)

13. What common English words have their origin in these place names?

Canterbury Cyprus Bayonne Damascus
Oporto Buncombe (N. Carolina) Tangiers Spain
Milan

14. Show the meanings of the following words by reference to the gods or goddesses from whose names they are derived:

(*a*)

atlas cereal jovial bacchanalian
fauna hectoring hygiene mentor
panic mercurial

(*b*)
martial protean saturnine vestal titanic
volcanic hermetic tantalize vulcanite stentorian

15. Can you say who gave their names to:

(*a*) these days of the week?
Tuesday Wednesday Thursday Friday Saturday

(*b*) these months of the year?
January March July August

16. Here are some words of Biblical origin. Can you explain them?

babel bedlam jeremiad lazaretto maudlin

17. These words have an 'aristocratic' origin:

brougham cardigan chesterfield petersham sandwich

What do they mean? With whose names are they associated?

18. What inventions or discoveries are associated with the names of?

L. H. Baekeland Galvani Dr. Guillotin
Joseph Hansom C. Macintosh Louis Pasteur
M. Daguerre Etienne de Silhouette
J. L. McAdam A. Sax

19. What common English words were derived from the names of these persons? –

(*a*) a 17th-century hangman
(*b*) a murderer, executed for smothering people whose bodies he sold for dissection
(*c*) an Irish land-agent who was ostracized by his tenants
(*d*) a German Count who invented a type of airship
(*e*) a Norwegian traitor who collaborated with the Nazis

20. New flowers and fruits are sometimes named after the people who discovered or introduced them. Can you say who gave their names to the following?

camellia	dahlia	fuchsia	greengage
godetia	lobelia	magnolia	loganberry
eschscholtzia	zinnia		

21. The names of certain fabrics are derived from their places of origin. Explain these:

arras	calico	cambric	diaper	gingham
melton	muslin	nankeen	tweed	worsted

22. What's the word for?

(*a*) a type of hat, named after a novel by George du Maurier
(*b*) a strict disciplinarian, named after a French drill-master of the reign of Louis XIV
(*c*) a magnificent tomb, named after a King of Caria (4th-century B.C.) for whom his queen built one
(*d*) a state of hypnotism, named after a Swiss physician (1733–1815) whose treatment was introduced as animal magnetism
(*e*) bullets packed in shells, named after the inventor, a general of the Peninsular War period
(*f*) the accidental confusion of words, named after a Warden of New College, Oxford (d. 1930)
(*g*) an outline portrait in profile, named after a French minister of finance (1709–67)
(*h*) a dye, named after a town in North Italy and discovered shortly after a battle there in 1859
(*i*) a kind of nonsense verse, named after a town in Ireland
(*j*) a stately mansion named after a hill in Rome on which Augustus built his house

23. What is a *patronymic?* Illustrate your answer by reference to the following names:

Robinson Pritchard Macdonald
Fitzherbert O'Donnell

24. What do you understand by the term *vogue words?* What twentieth-century connotations have the following words acquired?

(*a*) appeasement (*b*) blueprint (*c*) liquidate
(*d*) sanctions (*e*) totalitarian

25. Certain familiar expressions (known to purists as 'elegancies') have their origin in the opinion of those who use them that they are more genteel or elegant than the terms they displace. Can you say what is meant by the following?

(*a*) to perform one's ablutions
(*b*) the festive board
(*c*) in the lower income bracket
(*d*) floral tributes
(*e*) at the highest level

2

WHAT'S THE WORD ?

You have it on 'the tip of your tongue'? But how often do you find that the word you want, the *mot juste*, eludes you at the very moment when you want it?

Proficiency in the use of English depends primarily on the possession of an adequate vocabulary. Here are some questions which will help you to assess your basic equipment and build up your stock of words:

1. You have in mind an idea, a phrase, which you know can be expressed in a single word. What *is* the word? Can you find it for each of these phrases?

(*a*) a citizen of the world
(*b*) length of life
(*c*) correctness of behaviour
(*d*) worthy of praise
(*e*) the prevailing fashion
(*f*) of strong health and physique
(*g*) to soak in a liquid
(*h*) to reduce to powder or dust
(*i*) shaped like a cross
(*j*) indented like a saw

2. Give one word for each phrase:

(*a*) to separate into parts
(*b*) to turn to stone
(*c*) without blemish
(*d*) done by stealth
(*e*) lasting only a day
(*f*) violation of what is sacred
(*g*) to blot out
(*h*) a display of fireworks
(*i*) belonging to familiar speech
(*j*) swearing to a statement known to be false

3. One word for each phrase:

(*a*) that cannot be felt
(*b*) that cannot be avoided
(*c*) that cannot be wounded
(*d*) that cannot be rubbed out

(*e*) that cannot be satisfied
(*f*) that cannot be taken by arms
(*g*) that cannot be touched
(*h*) that cannot be understood
(*i*) that cannot be seen
(*j*) that cannot be heard

4. One word for each phrase:

(*a*) a yearly allowance
(*b*) a reading-desk in church
(*c*) a literary theft
(*d*) a declaration upon oath
(*e*) a note to help the memory
(*f*) a medicine to cause vomiting
(*g*) an animal that chews the cud
(*h*) a person engaged for all kinds of work
(*i*) a person authorised to act for another
(*j*) a new word formed by transposing the letters of the original word

5. One word for each phrase:

(*a*) to cut off the head
(*b*) to free from blame
(*c*) a general pardon
(*d*) a pattern of excellence
(*e*) one who kills a king
(*f*) correct in doctrine
(*g*) relating to the eye
(*h*) the art of making speeches
(*i*) to surrender on terms
(*j*) to make a preliminary survey of enemy territory

6. What names are given to these sciences or studies? (Each word has the ending – *logy*; e.g. Mythology – the study of myths.)

(*a*) The study of man as an animal (a..........)
(*b*) The study of antiquities (a..........)
(*c*) The science of physical life (b......)
(*d*) The study of insects (e.........)
(*e*) The science of birds (o..........)
(*f*) The science of races and their relationships (e........)
(*g*) The science of the soul or mind (p.........)
(*h*) The study of handwriting (g.........)
(*i*) The art of bell-ringing (c..........)
(*j*) The science of the industrial arts (t ....)

7. Can you name these arts or studies? Each word has the ending, *-graphy*.

(*a*) The written account of a life (b........)
(*b*) The designing of ballet (c...........)
(*c*) Map-drawing (c..........)
(*d*) The science of the earth's surface (g........)
(*e*) The art of engraving on stone (l..........)
(*f*) The recording of earthquakes (s...........)
(*g*) The writing of saints' lives (h..........)
(*h*) The describing and mapping of a place or district (t.........)
(*i*) A description of books, especially those dealing with a particular subject (b...........)
(*j*) The art of producing pictures by the action of light on sensitive film (p..........)

8. What names are given to the occupations of these people? (Each word ends in *-ist*.)

(*a*) He plays an instrument in support of a singer (a..........)
(*b*) He studies plants (b.......)
(*c*) He specialises in the treatment of your feet and hands (c..........)
(*d*) He writes plays (d........)
(*e*) He writes for the newspapers (j.........)
(*f*) He studies and collects coins (n..........)
(*g*) He is an eye-doctor (o......)
(*h*) He collects postage-stamps (p..........)
(*i*) He preserves and mounts the skins of animals (t..........)
(*j*) He studies the production and distribution of wealth (e........)

9. What do we call these ruling classes? (Each word ends in *-cracy*.)

(*a*) A ruling body of nobles or privileged people
(*b*) Government by an absolute ruler

(*c*) Government by officials and red-tape
(*d*) Government by the people
(*e*) The rule of the wealthy

10. What people would you expect to find in these groups?

(*a*) a bench of - - - - -
(*b*) a board of - - - - -
(*c*) a conclave of - - - -
(*d*) a panel of - - - - -
(*e*) a posse of - - - - -

11. Can you give the Group Names (or Nouns of Multitude) for these animals?

(*a*) a - - - - of cattle
(*b*) a - - - - - of sheep
(*c*) a - - - - of pups
(*d*) a - - - - - of hounds
(*e*) a - - - - - of rabbits

12. And for these birds?

(*a*) a - - - - - of quails
(*b*) a - - - - of rooks
(*c*) a - - - - - of partridges
(*d*) a - - - - of geese

13. For what birds are the following group names used?

(*a*) a *desert* of - - - -
(*b*) a *muster* of - - - -
(*c*) a *nide* of - - - -
(*d*) a *wisp* of - - - -

14. What is the difference between these words when used as group names?

(*a*) cast – caste
(*b*) troop – troupe

15. Can you complete these less familiar nouns of multitude for animals?

(*a*) a d - - - of hares
(*b*) a c - - - of badgers
(*c*) a k - - - - - of kittens
(*d*) a l - - - of leopards
(*e*) a p - - - of asses

16. Here are some jumbled group names. Can you put them right?

(*a*) a pride of foxes
(*b*) a school of bears
(*c*) a skulk of hogs
(*d*) a sounder of whales
(*e*) a sleuth of lions

17. Complete the nouns of multitude in group (*a*) by choosing words from group (*b*):

(*a*)	shoal	horde	stud	herd	nest
	batch	bunch	chest	clutch	flight
(*b*)	horses	bread	eggs	beakers	savages
	grapes	drawers	herrings	buffaloes	steps

18. Treat these in the same way:

(*a*)	library	fell	swarm	galaxy	skein
	fleet	stand	watch	clump	siege (sedge)
(*b*)	stars	thread	hair	ships	books
	plovers	herons	trees	bees	nightingales

19. Can you find a synonym ending in *-id* for each of the following?

(*a*) parched, barren
(*b*) frank, unbiased
(*c*) cold, chilling
(*d*) clear, bright
(*e*) unwholesome, diseased
(*f*) rotten, decomposed
(*g*) swift, speedy
(*h*) stinking, like stale fat
(*i*) not clear, muddy
(*j*) flat, tasteless

20. Find a verb ending in *-ate* for each of these meanings:

(*a*) to foreshadow, represent in outline (a . . . . . ate)
(*b*) to chastise (c . . . . . ate)
(*c*) to defame, blacken (d . . . . . ate)
(*d*) to tear up by the roots (e . . . . . ate)
(*e*) to thunder (in censure) (f . . . . . ate)
(*f*) to remain asleep during winter (h . . . . . ate)
(*g*) to make clear by examples (i . . . . . . ate)

(*h*) to go to law, contest at law (l . . . . ate)
(*i*) to mention by name, propose for election (n . . . . ate)
(*j*) to bring or come to an end (t . . . . . ate)

21. And for these?

(*a*) to amass, heap up (a . . . . . . ate)
(*b*) to clot, curdle (c . . . . . ate)
(*c*) to sow, scatter abroad (d . . . . ate)
(*d*) to set free (e . . . . . . ate)
(*e*) to whirl, revolve (g . . ate)
(*f*) to oil, make slippery (l . . . . . ate)
(*g*) to adjust, regulate (m. . . . ate)
(*h*) to proclaim, make known to the public (p . . . . . . ate)
(*i*) to repair, make new again (r . . . . ate)
(*j*) to waver, move from side to side (v . . . . . ate)

22. Give a noun ending in *-tude* for each of these meanings:

(*a*) fitness, natural ability (a . . . tude)
(*b*) blessedness (b . . . . tude)
(*c*) enfeeblement through age or infirmities (d . . . . . . tude)
(*d*) thankfulness (g . . . . tude)
(*e*) foolishness, absurdity (i . . . . . tude)
(*f*) breadth, freedom from narrowness (l . . . tude)
(*g*) commonplace remark (p . . . . tude)
(*h*) repose, calmness, rest (q . . . tude)
(*i*) feeling of anxiety, concern (s . . . . . tude)
(*j*) change of fortune, circumstances (v . . . . . . tude)

23. Add a prefix to each of the following words to give a word of opposite meaning:

official	definite	literate	common	normal
courteous	moral	legible	resolute	possible
delicate	noble	penitent	arrange	fashionable
applicable	mortal	reverent	veil	sense

24. Find a *synonym* in group (B) for each of the words in group (A):

A.

arduous	bucolic	chagrin	dissolute	emolument
jocund	germane	immanent	fortuitous	hypothetical
latent	mercurial	noisome	opprobrium	peccant
quandary	repletion	succinct	temerity	vituperate

B.

erring	inherent	merry	volatile	relevant
dormant	revile	terse	dilemma	conjectural
satiety	rashness	profit	vexation	accidental
disgrace	pastoral	laborious	offensive	licentious

25. Find an *antonym* (a word of opposite meaning) for each of the words in group (A). Select from (B):

A.

anomalous	brusque	clandestine	zeal
fecundity	garrulous	impecunious	equity
hilarity	malodorous	opaque	permanent
reconcile	theoretical	solitary	winsome
deleterious	lugubrious	nonchalant	veracious

B.

gregarious	sterility	apathy	fragrant
temporary	beneficial	manifest	false
effusive	regular	estrange	melancholy
unattractive	taciturn	injustice	cheerful
excited	transparent	affluent	practical

26. Give the adjectives corresponding to the following (e.g. noun – *passion*; adjective – *passionate*.)

advantage	burglar	comparison	discipline	essence
fraud	glass	humour	instrument	joke
knight	laity	mettle	nose	oracle
parish	qualm	remedy	spleen	title
utility	vandal	worship	yeast	zone

27. What manner of MAN is this? (In this exercise and those which follow it, you are asked to give a group of words all of which begin with the same three letters. The meaning of each word is provided and the number of letters indicated. Can you supply the words without reference to a dictionary?):

MAN . . . . – person in charge of a business
MAN . . . . . – buyer of provisions for a college
MAN . . . . . – Chinese official
MAN . . . . . . – person employed to show off garments
MAN . . . . – a little man

28. A lucky DIP? Can you supply the words required from the clues provided?

DIP . . . . – an official document; a degree certificate
DIP . . . – a kind of bird
DIP . . . . . – a clever negotiator
DIP . . . . – a craving for alcohol
DIP . . . . – an ancient writing-tablet

29. Out of the PAN:

PAN . . . . – confusion, uproar
PAN . . . . . . – a speech full of praise
PAN . . . . – a pompous official
PAN . . . . . – unbroken view of a region
PAN . . . . – van for removal of furniture; warehouse for furniture

30. Having FUN? Have some more – with these:

FUN . . . – ship's chimney
FUN . . . . . – dark and dismal
FUN . . . . – basic
FUN . . . . . . – may be a mushroom killer
FUN . . . . – an official

31. All FUR –

FUR . . . . – to polish up, renovate
FUR . . . . . . – usually accompanied by frills
FUR . . . . . – soldier's leave of absence
FUR . . . . – once a furrow's length; now fraction of a mile
FUR . . . . – stealthy, sly

32. What kind of CAR?

CAR . . . . – a great slaughter
CAR . . . . – pertaining to the heart
CAR . . . . . . – a precious stone or a fiery tumour
CAR . . . . – flesh-eating
CAR . . . . – fortune-telling by playing-cards

33. If you CAN – say what these are:

CAN . . . . . . – he may be elected
CAN . . . . . . – a solicitor of votes
CAN . . . . . – a little song, a hymn
CAN . . . . – quarrelsome
CAN . . . . . . – a kind of melon

34. If the CAP fits . . .

CAP . . . . – guided by whim or fancy
CAP . . . . . – holding-power
CAP . . . . – fee of so much a head
CAP . . . . . . – to charm
CAP . . . . – head or cornice of pillar

35. And these at the END:

END . . . . . . – a permanent income bequeathed to a person
END . . . . – to sign one's name on the back of a cheque
END . . . . . – acting on the skin
END . . . – kind of chicory used as salad
END . . . . – lining membrane of the heart

3

WHAT DOES IT MEAN ?

To say that we know the word we want, or that we have it on the tip of the tongue, does not necessarily imply that we fully understand what it means. Obviously the word cannot truly be claimed as part of our 'stock in trade' if its connotations are not clear. Confusion is often caused through a speaker's ignorance of the difference in meaning between words of similar sound and spelling. (Do you know, for example, what Mrs Malaprop meant when she spoke of 'a nice *derangement* of *epitaphs*'?)

Here are some questions to test your powers of discrimination:

1. Many words have changed in meaning with the passage of time. In some cases, this has resulted in what might be called a lowering of their dignity; in others, there has been a rise in reputation.

Can you give three different meanings for each of the following? Number the meanings in order of development:

(*a*) cash (*b*) conceit (*c*) delicate (*d*) imp (*e*) nice

2. Explain the italic words in the following expressions, showing how they have changed in meaning:

(*a*) the *quick* and the dead
(*b*) the *silly* sheep
(*c*) every man in his *humour*

3. Here are three words that have enhanced their reputation with the passing of time. Can you give their original meanings?

(*a*) chamberlain (*b*) knight (*c*) minister

4. These words have suffered a loss of dignity as they have changed in meaning. Can you give (i) the original meaning, and (ii) the present meaning for each?

(*a*) caitiff (*b*) knave (*c*) idiot (*d*) libertine

5. Can you show the connection between *humour* and *melancholy* by reference to the original meanings of these words? (See question 2, *c*.)

6. Supply the missing letters in the following words:

WORD	ORIGINAL MEANING	PRESENT MEANING
(*a*) M.....	a half	a small part
(*b*) V	in general use	coarse
(*c*) G	well-born, noble	liberal
(*d*) U	unknown	uncultured
(*e*) S	sharp, caustic	astute, sensible

7. Can you find the words indicated by the following clues? –

(*a*) It means *relish* or *gusto* now, but formerly denoted peel used to make wines more piquant.
(*b*) This *heathen* was once simply a man of the country.
(*c*) Now used for any kind of *success*, it once implied a victor's procession.

8. What qualities or characteristics were once described by these adjectives?

(*a*) brave (*b*) fond (*c*) sad

9. Give the modern word or phrase for each of these archaisms:

anent burthen enow forbears naught
albeit perchance welkin howbeit methought

10. Here are two pairs of words which have declined in reputation. By reference to their original meanings, suggest reasons for the change:

(*a*) artful – crafty (*b*) erring – vagabond

11. Supply the missing letters:

	WORD	ORIGINAL MEANING	PRESENT MEANING
(*a*)	E . . . A . . G . . T	– wandering be-yond bounds	– wasteful, immoderate
(*b*)	C . N . S . R .	– a constellation (the 'Little Bear')	– a centre of attraction
(*c*)	F . L . I . A . E	– to thunder	– censure, issue threats
(*d*)	E . C . N . R . C	– not having axis placed centrally	– odd, irregular
(*e*)	O . F . C . O . S	– obliging	– meddlesome, intrusive

12. In the following exercises, you are asked to distinguish between words that are similar in spelling though different in meaning.

The words in these pairs differ by only *one* letter. Complete the spellings so that each word is followed by the correct definition:

	WORD	*MEANING*
(*a*)	ALL . Y	to alleviate, diminish
	ALL . Y	to debase, mix with baser metal
(*b*)	CONV . Y	to carry, transport, communicate
	CONV . Y	to escort with armed force
(*c*)	F . CTITIOUS	artificial, not natural
	F . CTITIOUS	imaginary, unreal, counterfeit
(*d*)	REVEREN .	worthy of reverence
	REVEREN .	showing or feeling reverence
(*e*)	SP . CIOUS	roomy
	SP . CIOUS	plausible

13. Supply *one* letter for each word:

(*a*) AUG . R — instrument for boring holes
AUG . R — soothsayer, foreteller of future events
(*b*) CENS . R — vessel in which incense burnt
CENS . R — official judging morals, conduct, etc.
(*c*) INGEN . OUS — showing skill in contriving
INGEN . OUS — artless, frank, innocent
(*d*) MEND . CITY — lying, untruthfulness
MEND . CITY — begging, living on alms
(*e*) . ESSION — surrendering rights, giving up
. ESSION — period during which meetings held

14. Supply *one* letter for each word:

(*a*) AS . ENT — a rise, movement upward
AS . ENT — sanction, expression of agreement
(*b*) COMPL . MENT — number required to complete
COMPL . MENT — formal greetings, expression of praise
(*c*) LE . ITY — frivolity
LE . ITY — mercifulness
(*d*) STATION . RY — not moving
STATION . RY — writing materials
(*e*) V . CATION — holiday
V . CATION — profession, calling

15. These words have *two* letters different. Can you supply them?

(*a*) ASTRO . O . Y — study of the heavenly bodies
ASTRO . O . Y — science (so-called) of predicting events by the stars
(*b*) BRID . . — belonging to a bride, wedding
BRID . . — reins, etc., to guide a horse
(*c*) FORM . . LY — in an earlier period
FORM . . LY — in a conventional manner
(*d*) MON . T . RY — warning
MON . T . RY — financial; belonging to the coinage
(*e*) . YMB . L — a musical instrument
. YMB . L — token or sign

16. Supply *three* letters for each word:

(*a*)	ANO . . . OUS	abnormal, irregular
	ANO . . . OUS	of unknown authorship
(*b*)	D . . . ENT	downward slope or motion
	D . . . ENT	disagreement, difference of opinion
(*c*)	EPIT . . .	abridgement, summary; condensed account
	EPIT . . .	inscription on a tomb
(*d*)	JUNCT . . .	a meeting-place
	JUNCT . . .	concurrence of events; critical point of time
(*e*)	MOMENT . . .	of serious import
	MOMENT . . .	transitory, short-lived

17. Which is the man of influence?

(*a*) martial – marshal
(*b*) principal – principle
(*c*) tycoon – typhoon

What do the other words mean?

18. In each of the following exercises, you are asked to complete the phrase in brackets with one of the paired words. The meanings of all the discarded words should be checked.

(*a*)	alternate – alternative		(an - - - - - - - choice)
(*b*)	annalist – analyst		(ingredients checked by the - - - - - - -)
(*c*)	ascetic – acetic		(his - - - - - - - habits)
(*d*)	apprised – appraised		(- - - - - - - of the news)
(*e*)	apostate – apostle		(written by the - - - - - - - St John)

19. Choose the correct word for the phrase:

(*a*)	congenial – congenital	(a - - - - - - - disease)
(*b*)	corporal – corporeal	(abolish - - - - - - - punishment)
(*c*)	continual – continuous	(these - - - - - - - interruptions)
(*d*)	credible – credulous	(a very - - - - - - - story)
(*e*)	courtesy – curtsy	(treated with - - - - - - -)

20. Choose the correct word for the phrase:

(*a*) defective – deficient (food - - - - - - - in protein)
(*b*) definitive – definite (a - - - - - - - edition of his works)
(*c*) deposition – disposition (the - - - - - - - of their troops)
(*d*) deprecate – depreciate (we - - - - - - - such haste)
(*e*) difference – deference (in - - - - - - - to the bishop's wishes)

21. Choose the correct word for the phrase:

(*a*) efficient – efficacious (an - - - - - - - secretary)
(*b*) elemental – elementary (text-book on - - - - - - - Science)
(*c*) epigram – epigraph (an - - - - - - - from his witty play)
(*d*) erratic – erroneous (the stream's - - - - - - - course)
(*e*) expedient – expeditious (it is - - - - - - - that they resign)

22. Choose the correct word:

(*a*) fluent – fluid (a - - - - - - - maiden speech)
(*b*) factious – fractious (this - - - - - - - child)
(*c*) fallible – fallacious (we are all - - - - - - -)
(*d*) felicity – facility (live in contentment and - - - - - - -)
(*e*) floral – florid (admiring the - - - - - - - decorations)

23. Choose the correct word:

(*a*) imaginary – imaginative (an - - - - - - - conversation)
(*b*) imperial – imperious (his - - - - - - - crown)
(*c*) indignant – indigent (food for - - - - - - - refugees)
(*d*) inflammable – inflammatory (your - - - - - - - remarks)
(*e*) innocent – innocuous (the snake-bites were - - - - - - -)

24. Choose the correct word:

(*a*) judicial – judicious (a - - - - - - - assembly)
(*b*) jurisdiction – jurisprudence (not within his - - - - - - -)
(*c*) liniment – lineament (use the - - - - - - - twice daily)

(*d*) licentiate – licentious (a wild, - - - - - - - young man)
(*e*) liquefy – liquidate (trying to - - - - - - - his debts)

25 Choose the correct word:

(*a*) medicate – meditate (to - - - - - - - on this subject)
(*b*) meritorious– meretricious (an affected, - - - - - - - style)
(*c*) notable – notorious (a most - - - - - - - gangster)
(*d*) ordinance – ordnance (an - - - - - - - survey map)
(*e*) observance – observation (your powers of - - - - - - -)

26. Choose the correct word:

(*a*) perspicacity – perspicuity (his shrewdness and - - - - - - -)
(*b*) plaintive – plaintiff (a solemn, - - - - - - - tune)
(*c*) practical – practicable (not a - - - - - - - suggestion)
(*d*) presumptive – presumptuous (the heir - - - - - - -)
(*e*) punctual – punctilious (a - - - - - - - concern for details)

27. Choose the correct word:

(*a*) recourse – resource (having - - - - - - - to this plan)
(*b*) refectory – refractory (tea in the - - - - - - -)
(*c*) regulate – relegate (to - - - - - - - to a lower form)
(*d*) repertory – repertoire (her - - - - - - - of songs)
(*e*) revelation – revolution (a - - - - - - - of divine will)

28. Choose the correct word:

(*a*) sanguine – sanguinary (a man of - - - - - - - temperament)
(*b*) sensitive – sensuous (always - - - - - - - to criticism)
(*c*) social – sociable (a - - - - - - - congregation)
(*d*) stimulus – stimulant (a - - - - - - - before his meal)
(*e*) superficial – supercilious (a - - - - - - - sneer)

29. Choose the correct word:

(*a*) temperate – temporal (in a - - - - - - - zone)
(*b*) testament – testimony (my last will and - - - - - - -)
(*c*) topical – typical (song with - - - - - - - allusions)
(*d*) transitive – transitory (this - - - - - - - life)
(*e*) turbid – turgid (the - - - - - - - pool)

30. Choose the correct word:

(*a*) ulterior – ultimate (with no - - - - - - - motive)
(*b*) urban – urbane (an elegant, - - - - - - - manner)
(*c*) verbal – verbose (his boring, - - - - - - - writings)
(*d*) volatile – voluble (a - - - - - - -, convincing speaker)
(*e*) warrant – warranty (a - - - - - - - for the search)

31. Can you say how the words in the following groups differ in meaning and usage?

(*a*) assure – ensure – insure
(*b*) credence – credentials – credit
(*c*) euphemism – euphony – euphuism
(*d*) primal – primary – primitive
(*e*) respective – respectable – respectful

32. What difference in meaning and usage is made by the addition of a letter to the second word in each of these pairs?

(*a*) artist – artiste
(*b*) ay – aye
(*c*) cord – chord
(*d*) by – bye
(*e*) forgo – forego
(*f*) human – humane
(*g*) loose – loosen
(*h*) moral – morale
(*i*) wake – awake
(*j*) wave – waive

33. Here are more pairs of words that look alike. Show that you can distinguish between them:

(*a*) adverse – averse
(*b*) distinct – distinctive
(*c*) economic – economical
(*d*) historic – historical
(*e*) precipitate – precipitous
(*f*) advice – advise
(*g*) childish – childlike
(*h*) effectual – effective
(*i*) indict – indite
(*j*) venal – venial

34. These, too:

(*a*) affect – effect
(*b*) councillor – counsellor
(*c*) delusion – illusion
(*d*) elicit – illicit
(*e*) reversal– reversion
(*f*) decided – decisive
(*g*) exceeding – excessive
(*h*) lifelong – livelong
(*i*) purport – purpose
(*j*) virtual – virtuous

35. The following words are often misused in speech and writing. Can you say what errors are likely to be made?

aggravate	awfully	between	chronic	due
hectic	literally	mutual	nice	transpire

36. You are now invited to look at some words which you have probably never seen before, unless you happen to be a solver of erudite crossword puzzles or a setter of problems for radio panel games. Though they are all to be found in a good dictionary, they are not words which form part of the average reader's vocabulary. Don't let this intimidate or discourage you. You may regard the exercise as 'for entertainment only', though its main purpose is to illustrate the interesting discoveries one can make when delving in the dictionary.

Examine carefully the ten words given below and the definitions with which they have been wrongly paired. Can you say (deduce or guess) what the words mean, and link them with the correct meanings?

Ataraxy – mob rule
Bort – coarse sacking
Compotation – difficulty in breathing
Dyspnoea – shunning daylight
Gunny – diamond fragments made in cutting
Guttate – ravine, deep narrow valley in South Africa
Kloof – a diving, fish-eating duck
Lucifugous – speckled
Merganser – tippling, drinking together
Ochlocracy – stoical indifference

37. Re-arrange similarly these words and definitions to show the correct meanings:

Eupeptic – gifted with prophetic power
Fatidical – carved on the surface
Glabrous – having good digestion
Hepatic – smooth-skinned, free from hair
Hircine – good for the liver
Intagliated – goat-like
Malm – a retaining wall
Nenuphar – soft, chalky rock, soil from it
Revetment – stiff neck
Torticollis – a water lily

38. How do the following terms differ in meaning?
(*a*) murder (*b*) manslaughter (*c*) homicide

39. Distinguish between the two words:
(*a*) 'infer' and 'imply' (*b*) 'inherent' and 'innate'

40. (*a*) What is the difference between *prostrate* and *supine*? (In a well-known hymn, the worshipper anticipates the joy of meeting his Maker in the following lines:

'. . . What rapture will it be
Prostràte before thy throne to lie,
And gaze, and gaze on thee.'

Can you explain his predicament?)

(*b*) How does an *agnostic* differ from an *atheist*?

4

HOW DO YOU SPELL IT ?

As a mongrel language, English has been called 'the delight of etymologists and the despair of aliens'. English spelling standards, in particular, are notoriously inconsistent, and so confusing that they often remain the despair of natives, as well as aliens, who have tried in vain to understand them.

There are many aids to spelling, and many exceptions to the few rules or guiding principles that exist. Spelling 'bees' and word games may help. Small groups of linked or associated words are easier to learn than long lists of isolated ones. A careful study of homophones (words identical in sound but different in spelling and meaning) is recommended as an excellent way to begin your attack on the spelling bogy. (Or should it be *bogey*?)

1. Can you give a word which sounds the same but is spelt differently for each of the following?

aisle	braid	curb	Dane	draught
fair	Greece	heart	him	lock
muse	mean	nay	our	plum
pole	rest	side	tract	thrown

2. Give a word identical in sound but different in spelling and meaning for each of these words:

adds	brooch	crews	dew	fate
guild	hall	kernel	leek	manner
peer	quire	root	sheer	tray
use	vale	waist	yoke	key

3. There are three homophones in each of these groups. Given the meanings, can you supply the different spellings for each group?

(*a*) *i.* the eldest son	*ii.* what we breathe	*iii.* before
(*b*) *i.* to quote	*ii.* what is seen	*iii.* a position
(*c*) *i.* not fine	*ii.* a dead body	*iii.* ground for racing
(*d*) *i.* a temple	*ii.* to pretend	*iii.* willing(ly)
(*e*) *i.* a colour	*ii.* a person's name	*iii.* to cut
(*f*) *i.* come together	*ii.* food	*iii.* to measure
(*g*) *i.* a fruit	*ii.* two	*iii.* to peel
(*h*) *i.* to make marks	*ii.* not wrong	*iii.* a workman
(*i*) *i.* gratitude	*ii.* does pray	*iii.* takes as plunder
(*j*) *i.* a weather cock	*ii.* proud	*iii.* a blood vessel

4. Do you spell by the 'look and say' method? Try your hand at these words. Can you say without hesitation which is the correct spelling?

awful – aweful	desiccated – dessicated
library – libary	medecine – medicine
obligatto – obbligato	pursuade – persuade
radience – radiance	seperate – separate
stupify – stupefy	teetotaller – teatotaller

5. How many mistakes can you find in these spellings?

reconnaissance	physisist	succesful	riveted
quarreling	Piccadily	picallili	moccasin
connoiseur	committee	embarass	guarantee
disatisfied	accesibility	occurrence	professional
paralelled	supercilious	succulent	vaccinate

6. Find the Odd Man Out. One word in each group is wrongly spelt:

(*a*)	apopthegm	broccoli	colossal	diphthong
(*b*)	ecstasy	fidgetty	gymkhana	acquiesce
(*c*)	innocuous	jewellery	khaki	langorous
(*d*)	manoeuvre	naphtha	odyssey	properganda
(*e*)	innoculate	rarefy	tyranny	inveigle
(*f*)	ubiquitous	varigated	wilful	zephyr
(*g*)	vacillate	metallurgy	miscellany	transcendant
(*h*)	deteriorate	mischevious	decimate	inflammable
(*i*)	resusitate	poignancy	rhapsody	vicarious
(*j*)	serrated	gossamer	honary	development

7. Can you spell your ailment? – How many of these are incorrect . . . ?

asthma	bronchitis	catarrh	diarhoea
appendicitis	diptheria	erysipilas	fibrositis
dyspepsya	haemorrhage	jaundise	laryngitis
pnuemonia	influenza	meningitus	lumbago
quinsey	rheumatism	sciatica	tonsilitis

8. Are all these words spelled right?

slanderous	dextrous	idolatrous	thundrous
disasterous	murderous	cumbrous	boisterous
lustrous	monstrous		

9. Certain words may be spelt in two different ways. Can you give the second way of spelling each of these?

biased	burnt	cipher	connection	enquiry
focussing	gipsy	hiccup	jail	pigmy

10. How are these words spelt in the plural?

antenna	bacillus	dogma	formula	grotto
octopus	neurosis	genius	salvo	trousseau

11. Should 'i' come before 'e'? How many mistakes are there here?

bier	deceit	freize	sieze	wield
tier	weir	mein	relief	

12. Do you make an *acknowledgment* or an *acknowledgement*? Do you pass *judgement* or *judgment* ?
Can you comment on this point?

13. These words are often wrongly spelt? Can you say what mistakes are likely to be made?

aeroplane	business	asphalt	gauge	fuchsia
gramophone	parliament	government	sincerely	villain

14. Can you supply a silent letter to complete the spelling of each of these words?

a . moner	bom . er	condi . n	de . tor	. nome
.sychology	. nemonic	. tarmigan	. eirloom	. nout

15. Which of the following spellings are correct or to be recommended?

(*a*) cocoanut – cokernut – coconut
(*b*) aery – eyrie – aerie – eyry
(*c*) doily – doyly – doiley
(*d*) chute – shute – shoot
(*e*) melodion – melodeon – melodium

16. How many of the names of these musical instruments are wrongly spelt?

accordian	bassoon	chello	clarinette	guitar
harmonium	piccolo	saxaphone	ukalele	voilin

17. Can you spell the new word formed when the suffix indicated in brackets is added?

ache (-ing)	argue (-ment)	annul (-ment)
beauty (-fy)	humour (-ous)	pity (-ous)
rely (-able)	transfer (-ing)	use (-able)
waste (-ful)		

18. How many of these proper names are incorrectly spelt?

Aaron	Buddah	Ceasar	Epstein	Grieg
Galilio	Mendlessohn	Pharaoh	Schubert	Tchaekovski

19. How do you spell the words indicated by these shortened forms?

4th	9th	12th	18th	21st
30th	44th	58th	67th	99th

20. Can you add the correct ending (*ary*, *-ery* or *ory*)?

arch . . .	bound . . .	custom . . .	direct . . .
element . . .	fact . . .	gran . . .	honor . . .
invent . . .	jewell . . .		

21. Complete the names of these animals:

arm	buf	che	dro . . . . . .
gir	hip	hy . . .	jac . . .
kan	opo	rhi	

22. Which is the correct ending (*-eon*, *-ion* or *ian*)?

clar . . .	bludg . . .	guard . . .	bun . . .	gall . . .
surg . . .	custod . . .	music . . .	carr . . .	obliv . . .

23. The terminations *-ety* and *ity* are sometimes confused. Use the correct ending to form a noun from each of these adjectives:

anxious	brutal	pious	agile	nice
active	sober	docile	gay	extreme

24. The long sound of 'o' (as in *told*) may be represented by the following spellings: *oa, oe, ou, ow*. Select the right one to complete each of these words:

c . . st	h . . s	p . . ltry	m . . n	m . . ld
thr . . s	kn . . s	. . th	. . n	f . . s

25. Supply the right ending (*-cal* or *-cle*):

arti . . .   bicy . . .   ici . . .   canti . . .   medi . . .
vehi . . .   tragi . . .   practi . . .   parti . . .   verti . . .

26. Fill in the vowels in this group of medical terms:

. n . . sth . t . c   c . s . . lty   d . s . . s .   chl . r . f . rm
m . ss . g .   . . ntm . nt   m . d . c . n .   phys . c . . n
d . . gn . s . s   st . r . l . s .

27. Supply the ending (*-om* or *-um*):

accust . .   fulcr . .   laburn . .   rostr . .   phant . .
decor . .   empori . .   idi . .   rans . .   tedi . .

28. What errors can you find in the spelling of these titles and designations?

ambassador   barronet   cardinal   deputy   excellensy
governer   consol   mayor   licenciate
superintendant

29. Are you liable to confuse the terminations *-cy* and *-sy*? Complete these words:

agen . .   argo . .   fluen . .   pleuri . .   clemen . .
courte . .   here . .   lepro . .   tenan . .   curren . .

30. Here are three like-sounding endings which may cause hesitation when spelling: *-een*, *-ene* and *-ine*. Show that you know which is required for each of these words:

brigant . . .   cant . . .   crinol . . .   gelat . . .   conv . . .
quarant . . .   superv . . .   contrav . . .   tambour . . .   libert . . .

31. And here are four (*-eat*, *-eet*, *-eit* and *ete*) to add to the speller's embarrassment. Can you select the right one for each of these words?

athl . . .	conc . . .	forf . . .	discr . . .	entr . . .
repl . . .	obsol . . .	secr . . .	compl . . .	eff . . .

32. How many of these musical terms are correctly spelt?

aria	cantarto	fugue	minuette	fantazia
gavote	rallentando	intermezzo	polonaise	staccato

5

HOW DO YOU SAY IT ?

A standard English pronunciation does not exist, despite attempts by fastidious writers from Swift to Shaw to establish one. We are as illogical in the way we say our words as in the way we spell them. Personal preferences, regional peculiarities, variants perpetrated by our English-speaking cousins overseas, and the gradual naturalization of imported foreign words and phrases have combined to make uniformity impossible. (A typical example of the resulting confusion is the pronunciation of the word *armada.* If you say ar-*mah*-da, as you probably do, you may be surprised to learn that the majority of dictionaries, and authorities such as the BBC Advisory Committee on Spoken English, recommend ar-*may*-da.)

The advice given by Fowler in *Modern English Usage* is: 'Pronounce as your neighbours do, not better; for words in general use, the general public is your neighbour.'

With this in mind, you are invited to test yourself in the following exercises:

1. Which pronunciation would you recommend for these words?

adieu (a-dew' or a-dee-eu'?)
abdomen (*ab*'-do-men or ab-*doh*'-men?)
epoch (*ep*'-ok or *ee*'-pok?)
robust (*roe*'-bust or roe-*bust*'?)
vase (vawz, vahz, or vayz?)

2. How many syllables do you make when pronouncing these words?

adobe	bourgeois	cerement	clerestory	extempore
extraordinary	furore	interesting	lineage	medicine

3. Which letter is silent in these words?

conduit	feoff	jeopardy	mortgage	posthumous
ragout	raspberry	rendezvous	seraglio	subtle

4. Here are some short but tricky words. Can you say them aloud without hesitation?

aeon	ague	balk	chagrin	ego
façade	fracas	helot	indict	lapel
mien	morale	naïve	orgy	posse
skein	ski	sieve	scone	tryst

5. Can you pronounce the names of these famous people?

Chekov	Dumas	Goethe	Wagner	Machiavelli
Mozart	Pepys	Picasso	Haydn	Xavier

6. How do you pronounce these vocational or professional names?

almoner	antiquary	architect	artificer	artiste
chauffeur	chiropodist	comptroller	commandant	executor
financier	glazier	gynaecologist	librarian	masseuse
metallurgist	ostler	seamstress	stevedore	victualler

7. These, too, are the names of types of people. How do you pronounce them?

aristocrat	capitalist	cicerone	connoisseur	dilettante
fakir	matriarch	plagiarist	premier	vizier

8. How do you pronounce the names of these flowers?

dahlia	anemone	clematis	cyclamen	edelweiss
eschscholtzia	hyacinth	marigold	pentstemon	viola

9. And the names of these birds?

egret	flamingo	guillemot	halcyon	osprey
plover	ptarmigan	throstle	wheatear	widgeon

10. And these animals?

camelopard	coyote	gnu	iguana	ibex
lemur	okapi	opossum	palfrey	zebra

11. How should these musical terms be pronounced?

appoggiatura	aria	arpeggio	cello	descant
fantasia	scenario	scherzo	viola	sonata

12. These foreign words and phrases are also in common use in English. Can you pronounce them?

(*a*)	albino	alibi	amoeba	bacillus	campanile
	clientele	début	façade	fungi	gala
		negligé(e)	nonpareil	subpoena	

(*b*)	a priori	bas relief	bona fide	chef d'ouvre
	coup d'état	cul-de-sac	faux pas	prima facie
	raison d'être	sang-froid	sine die	sotto voce
	table d'hôte	tête-à-tête	tout ensemble	

13. Can you say where the accent falls in the pronouncing of these adjectives?

applicable	clandestine	communal	comparable
conversant	decadent	decorous	despicable
disciplinary	disputable	doctrinal	exquisite
formidable	hospitable	illustrative	impious
irremediable	irreparable	lamentable	laudatory

14. And where does it fall in these?

maniacal	mischievous	momentary	nonchalant
numismatic	obdurate	obligatory	orthopaedic
preferable	posthumous	refutable	remediable
salutary	secretive	sedentary	sonorous
temporary	ubiquitous	vehement	vibratory

15. How should these nouns be pronounced?

acoustics	albumen	amenity
aspirant	auction	bravado
centenary	chastisement	chiaroscuro
controversy	courtesy	cynosure
dynast	enema	espionage

16. And these?

forehead	ghoul	glacier
gyroscope	harem	imbecile
inventory	laboratory	lather
longevity	machination	moccasin
panegyric	plaque	precedence

17. These, too?

profile	protégé	ptomaine	quandary
questionnaire	recognizance	respite	route
satiety	schedule	sinecure	sobriquet
solecism	tenet	tornado	urinal
vagary	verdigris	vitamin	waistcoat

18. A change in meaning, or in the grammatical function of a word (e.g. from verb to noun or adjective), may call for a change in its pronunciation. This usually involves the shifting of the accent from one syllable to another.

Can you indicate the two pronunciations of each word

in the two groups that follow, having regard to the two meanings given for each?

attribute – (*a*) a characteristic quality
(*b*) to ascribe or refer to
buffet – (*a*) a blow of the hand
(*b*) a sideboard
compact – (*a*) neatly packed, condensed
(*b*) lady's miniature vanity case
conflict – (*a*) to struggle, clash with
(*b*) a fight, collision
consort – (*a*) husband or wife
(*b*) to keep company with
consummate – (*a*) to complete, accomplish
(*b*) perfect, masterly
converse – (*a*) opposite, contrary
(*b*) to talk with
convict – (*a*) to prove guilty
(*b*) a condemned criminal
defile – (*a*) to pollute, make dirty
(*b*) a gorge, narrow
digest – (*a*) a compendium, summary
(*b*) to assimilate passage (food) etc.

19. Indicate two pronunciations for each of these words:

discount – (*a*) to leave out of account
(*b*) deduction from amount due
forte – (*a*) person's strong point
(*b*) musical direction (=loud)
frequent – (*a*) to go to habitually
(*b*) regular, often
gallant – (*a*) brave, chivalrous
(*b*) attentive to women
incense – (*a*) smoke of sweet-smelling spice
(*b*) make angry
invalid – (*a*) having no legal force
(*b*) a sick person
object – (*a*) express disapproval
(*b*) thing aimed at

project	– (*a*) a plan, scheme (*b*) to contrive, plan
salve	– (*a*) healing ointment (*b*) to save from loss (e.g. ship)
slough	– (*a*) a snake's cast skin (*b*) quagmire, swamp

20. *Is it 'Al-' or 'Awl-'?*

All the following words begin with the same two letters but custom has prescribed a lengthened initial vowel for some of them. Divide them into two groups, showing which of them have the approved pronunciation of '*awl-*';

albeit	albino	albumen	alchemy	alcove
alderman	almanac	almoner	almost	alphabet
altar	altercate	alternate	altitude	altruism

21. Do you say *loss* or *lawss*? Do you *pass* or *pahss*?

Comment on the use of the long or the short vowel sound in these and the following words, indicating in each case which pronunciation you approve. (N.B. Fowler's warning on the folly of aping gentility is especially relevant here.):

bath (or bahth?)	class (or clahss?)	coffee (or cawfee?)
cross (or crawss?)	dog (or dawg?)	glass (or glahss?)
grass (or grahss?)	lass (or lahss?)	laugh (laf or lahf?)
mass (or mahss?)	off (or awf?)	often (offn or aw'fn?)
path (or pahth?)	revolve (or revawlve?)	soft (or sawft?)

6

HOW'S YOUR GRAMMAR?

To this question, the modern student might well reply with another: 'Does it matter?' In a permissive age, when standards of all kinds are freely flouted, need we worry any more about Grammar? We no longer insist on a slavish adherence to rules which earlier generations of pedants held to be sacrosanct. In many of our schools, the study of formal grammar has been relegated to a minor role in the English syllabus.

The argument is clear. The function of Grammar (which is defined as 'the general term for the science of language') is to examine and explain how words are formed, inflected, spoken, written, and arranged in sentences. But people spoke and wrote the language long before they formulated rules for speech and writing. Grammar must be kept in its place as the servant, not the master or dictator of language. Language is always changing; the solecisms (grammatical errors) of yesterday may be the accepted idiom of to-day, sanctioned by 'common usage'.

At the same time, if we have a concern for the beauty and precision of 'good English', we should remember that there are grammatical laws which do not change, and violation of them cannot be justified or condoned. 'To deplore the misuse of words and phrases by lazy thinkers and slipshod writers is not pedantry.'

In each of the exercises in this section, a pair of sentences has been chosen to illustrate a common error in popular usage.

Can you say in each case which sentence is to be preferred, and what is wrong (according to the old rules) with the other sentence?

1. (*a*) Every room, attic, cellar and garage was searched by the police.
   (*b*) Every room, attic, cellar and garage were searched by the police.

2. (*a*) None of his old friends were able to help him.
   (*b*) None of his old friends was able to help him.

3. (*a*) Neither Miss England nor Miss France was successful in the contest.
   (*b*) Neither Miss England nor Miss France were successful in the contest.

4. (*a*) Your birth certificate as well as your passport is required.
   (*b*) Your birth certificate as well as your passport are required.

5. (*a*) I would never recommend those sort of films.
   (*b*) I would never recommend that sort of film.

6. (*a*) She's one of those girls who always look attractive.
   (*b*) She's one of those girls who always looks attractive.

7. (*a*) The two old campaigners always wrote to one another on the anniversary of the battle.
   (*b*) The two old campaigners always wrote to each other on the anniversary of the battle.

8. (*a*) Are there less children in the village school today?
   (*b*) Are there fewer children in the village school today?

9. (*a*) The tycoon's estate was divided between his three surviving children.
   (*b*) The tycoon's estate was divided among his three surviving children.

10. (*a*) If either of the brigands is seen, he will be shot.
    (*b*) If either of the brigands are seen, he will be shot.

11. (*a*) 'Nothing shall ever come between you and I,' he told her.
    (*b*) 'Nothing shall ever come between you and me,' he told her.

12. (*a*) I was introduced to the Chairman and the Vice-Chairman of the Company.
    (*b*) I was introduced to the Chairman and Vice-Chairman of the Company.

13. (*a*) Can you imagine him forgetting a date like that?
    (*b*) Can you imagine his forgetting a date like that?

14. (*a*) They are players who I think will one day be famous.
    (*b*) They are players whom I think will one day be famous.

15. (*a*) If you were him, what would you think of her conduct?
    (*b*) If you were he, what would you think of her conduct?

16. (*a*) Playing the guitar, his dog howled all the time.
    (*b*) While he was playing the guitar, his dog howled all the time.

17. (*a*) The secretary said he'd written back without delay.
    (*b*) The secretary said he'd wrote back without delay.

18. (*a*) Candidates are advised to carefully and methodically read the instructions.
    (*b*) Candidates are advised to read the instructions carefully and methodically.

19. (*a*) They used not to allow such goings-on here.
    (*b*) They didn't use to allow such goings-on here.

20. (*a*) If I was wrong, I'd be the first to admit it.
    (*b*) If I were wrong, I'd be the first to admit it.

21. (*a*) We never have and never will yield to threats.
    (*b*) We never have yielded and never will yield to threats.

22. (*a*) This margarine is as good as if not better than butter.
    (*b*) This margarine is as good if not better than butter.

23. (*a*) In competitive sport, one can't afford to rest on his laurels.
    (*b*) In competitive sport, one can't afford to rest on one's laurels.

24. (*a*) I can't stand the heat as she can.
    (*b*) I can't stand the heat like she can.

25. (*a*) He won't pay without he gets his money's worth.
    (*b*) He won't pay unless he gets his money's worth.

26. (*a*) The angler had only caught two small fish.
    (*b*) The angler had caught only two small fish.

27. (*a*) I will never be out of debt.
    (*b*) I shall never be out of debt.

28. (*a*) It was a most unique experience for all of us.
    (*b*) It was a unique experience for all of us.

29. (*a*) She said she would wear neither the red nor the blue dress at the party.
    (*b*) She said she would neither wear the red nor the blue dress at the party.

30. (*a*) The man as told me this is usually reliable.
    (*b*) The man who told me this is usually reliable.

31. (*a*) Due to the postal strike, I did not receive your letter in time.
    (*b*) Owing to the postal strike, I did not receive your letter in time.

32. (*a*) The reason why he fails to impress is that he lacks self-confidence.
    (*b*) The reason why he fails to impress is because he lacks self-confidence.

33. (*a*) In that there tree we found this here nest.
    (*b*) In that tree we found this nest.

34. (*a*) He says he don't believe it's yours.
    (*b*) He says he doesn't believe it's yours.

35. (*a*) It was he who did it.
    (*b*) It was him what done it.

36. (*a*) Will you try and mend the machine?
    (*b*) Will you try to mend the machine?

37. (*a*) Has he got a lot of friends?
    (*b*) Has he many friends?

38. (*a*) When dining out, he liked a drink between courses.
    (*b*) When dining out, he liked to drink between each course.

39. (*a*) Can I drive you home?
    (*b*) May I drive you home?

40. (*a*) I expected to have found the boys still in bed.
    (*b*) I expected to find the boys still in bed.

7

WHERE DO WE STOP ?

Punctuation has been called 'the art of knowing where to stop'. A device to facilitate smooth reading and make clear the meaning of what has been written, it prevents ambiguity and indicates stresses, pauses and breaks in the continuity of thought.

Overstopping is still a common fault in writing, though the lavish punctuation favoured by Dickens and other Victorian novelists is no longer in fashion. The full stop which announces the end of a sentence is obviously indispensable to good composition. The comma, the most frequently misused punctuation mark, should be sparingly but fastidiously employed, though never as a substitute for the full stop or the semicolon.

In spite of attempts to simplify or even eliminate some of them (Note, for example, Bernard Shaw's rejection of the apostrophe), you will find in contemporary writing all the familiar seven signs (full stop, colon, semi-colon, comma, question mark, exclamation mark, and dash), together with such devices as inverted commas, hyphens, brackets and apostrophes.

1. Can you name the punctuation signs used for the following purposes?

(*a*) to introduce a list or enumeration of items

(*b*) to mark an abbreviation or contraction

(*c*) to separate individual items in a list

(*d*) to indicate an abrupt expression of emotion, surprise or excitement

(*e*) to show the omission of a letter or letters in a word

(*f*) to link two or more words which together form a single compound word

(*g*) to enclose a quotation or a passage of direct speech

(*h*) to mark an interruption or sudden digression

(*i*) to indicate the title of a book (when italic type is not used).

(*j*) to mark a request or enquiry

2. How many full stops are required here? Can you read the passages aloud without preparation and make sense of them? Write them out with full punctuation:

(*a*) Why did you say I told you why I thought I had made myself clear to all I mean who were paying attention

(*b*) The old fashioned remedy of counting a flock of sheep that leisurely pass by the poet Wordsworth included in his sonnet to sleep as one of the ways in which he had tried to cure his insomnia

(*c*) He tried to run faster but couldn't do it on the fresh rise he nearly tripped and fell but kept up cresting the hump of the field he could see a tall screen of poplars and some willows in the fold below and forced himself limping down to them at the bottom was a stream.

3. Make two sentences of these passages and punctuate fully:

(*a*) He dressed in a pale blue shirt knitted black tie and a grey suit he added a topcoat the day showed every promise of sunshine but there was a chill wind.

(*b*) You are not concentrating Jones Butcher said you must hit with your mind as well as your muscles

(*c*) Hum mused the inspector stroking his chin by the way he continued I wonder whether life is extinct

(*d*) Why he asked innocently the black knight don't you trust him

(*e*) We er you er that is he tried again taking another step forward

4. Make one sentence and punctuate:

(*a*) My gardener we call him Bertie and his official designation is Albert Edward O'Shaughnessy was as had been anticipated conspicuous by his absence

(*b*) Through a skin diving mask or glass bottomed boat you look into a world of almost unbelievable beauty castle like coral formations precipices jewelled with sea fans and hung with exquisitely hued sea plants

(*c*) Another friend of that period was six foot Billy who ate regularly in the café downstairs a stranded Negro sailor from Troy Missouri who had either jumped ship or had lost his way

(*d*) It was a small square canvas labelled portrait of the artist by himself

(*e*) When their general wanted him to have the twenty four deserters executed as a warning to others he just went stubborn and said general there are already too many weeping widows in the united states

5. How many errors in punctuation can you find in these sentences?

(*a*) I make good money, unfortunately I have expensive tastes.

(*b*) You do'nt think its the first time, do you!

(*c*) Their's not to reason why,
Their's but to do and die. (as Tennyson wrote it.)

(*d*) Among the spectators at the garden party were some of the local V.I.P.s; the Mayor. the Town Clerk, the Borough Treasurer, and the Director of Education.

(*e*) The second man interrupted her 'Excuse me, madam but did I hear you say, "Where is the Metropole Hotel"?'

6. More trouble on the football field! Can you sort out the viewpoints in these reports? Show clearly how the meaning

of the sentence is altered by the changes in punctuation:

(*a*) The captain said the goalkeeper was letting the side down.

(*b*) The captain, said the goalkeeper, was letting the side down.

(*c*) The captain said the goalkeeper was letting the side down?

(*d*) The captain said: 'The goalkeeper was letting the side down?'

(*e*) 'The captain?' said the goalkeeper. 'Was letting the side down?'

7. The full stop is used frequently after initials and to mark abbreviations or contractions. (Note, however, that some authorities [e.g. Fowler's *Modern English Usage*] advocate the omission of the stop when the first and last letters of the word appear in the abbreviation).

Give the abbreviations for the following words:

(*a*) February Postscript Mister Company Baronet Oxford Yorkshire Manuscripts hundredweight Doctor

(*b*) What do these abbreviations mean? Write each word or phrase in full:

inst.	i.e.	C.O.D.	Esq.	LL.D.
G.O.M.	Messrs.	Q.E.D.	lbs.	viz.

8. Some modern associations or organisations are better known to the general public by their abbreviated names than by their full titles. What are the full titles of the following?

E.N.S.A.	E.E.C.	U.N.E.S.C.O.	U.N.O.	R.A.D.A.
O.H.M.S.	P.E.N.	N.A.A.F.I.	N.A.T.O.	N.A.L.G.O.

9. Examiners in English for the Associated Examining Board complain of the 'prevalence of writing in which sentences are improperly constructed when the comma is made to do duty for the heavier stops'. Examine the following passages and say which of the legitimate uses of the comma are exemplified or illustrated by them:

(*a*) 'Ships, towers, domes, theatres and temples lie
Open unto the fields and to the sky'

(*b*) 'Down, and down, and down, he sank and drowned . . .'

(*c*) Awaking, Rip van Winkle found himself in a strange new world.

(*d*) What right has he, he thought, to pass judgment on me?

(*e*) The lorries having been loaded, the pickets moved in to intercept them.

10. Point out examples of the misuse or misplacing of commas in these sentences:

(*a*) His new play, having been accepted for production, the author was disappointed at the delay.

(*b*) I met an old friend at the concert, we agreed to meet again on the following night.

(*c*) I told her that the lane, to the old mill, by the river, would take her to the cottage, where I was born.

(*d*) 'There's day and night, brother both sweet things; sun, moon, and stars all sweet things, there's likewise a wind on the heath'.

(*e*) The Chancellor, of the Exchequer, in his Budget Speech said that the new tax would mean an annual saving, of £25,850000.

11. Show that you are familiar with the uses of the colon and the semicolon by inserting the appropriate stop where necessary in the following sentences:

(*a*) Summing up, the judge said 'Members of the jury, I have to draw your attention to certain puzzling aspects of this case . . .'

(*b*) This county is bordered by five shires Yorkshire, Nottinghamshire, Leicestershire, Staffordshire and Cheshire.

(*c*) In the doorway stood a weedy youth flamboyantly dressed in scarlet velvet in his cap was a long, curling feather.

(*d*) Prizes were awarded as follows 1st, J. C. Brown 2nd, E. W. Smith 3rd, P. K. Jones.

(*e*) To err is human to forgive, divine.

12. Insert question marks and exclamation marks where required:—

(*a*) 'Oh, how it takes me back' said Marlene when the lights had gone up.

(*b*) Was he free Was he happy The question is absurd. Had anything been wrong, we should certainly have heard.

(*c*) So where should I go It was just a question of getting there – France Italy Greece I knew nothing at all about any of them.

(*d*) Did she say 'Look in the garage'

(*e*) 'Listen' he said, pulling me back. 'You're sure the door is locked'

13. The hyphen is a symbol indicating that two or more words are to be regarded as one. Where they have become one through popular usage, the hyphen is not required. In which of the following compound words would you use it?

ante room birth place bomb proof by law common sense cross section foot note guide book hall mark hay fever high road law suit life time post office quarter day sitting room snack bar son in law text book title deeds

14. There are no apostrophes in these sentences. Can you supply them?

(*a*) Mines a bitter lemon; whats yours?

(*b*) Theyre leaving theirs in St. Jamess Street.

(*c*) Youll find the boys, mens and womens toilets on the same floor.

(*d*) Cant you see its lost its labels?

(*e*) Charles says Sams sisters shops not for sale.

15. Here, unpunctuated, is a newspaper advertisement of a 'Superior Architecturally Designed Fully Centrally Heated Three Bedroomed Detached Bungalow' which is for sale. Punctuate the passage as it would appear in the notice:

Porch hall 20ft long polished hardwood floor cloaks cupboard through lounge with french window to slabbed porch dining room/kitchen 14ft×10ft all modern fittings luxurious bathroom including shower unit tarmacadam forecourt with drive way to brick built garage elegant wrought iron gate at side with entrance to compact landscaped rear garden.

16. Punctuate these advertisements:

(*a*) 19 . . Ford Capri 1600 GT Automatic one local owner attractively coloured in royal purple with black trim fully equipped with automatic transmission radio matching spot and foglights heated rear window etc taxed Dec and in first class condition throughout unrepeatable at only £ . . .

(*b*) Radios washing machines recorders we have them all we can arrange confidential terms with four years to pay tube guarantees speedy installation in fact everything a customer wants write or phone shockproof electrics

17. Punctuate, and set out as an excerpt from a work of fiction, this passage from a novel by Iris Murdoch:

After a pause he said I'll tell you something very strange go on said dora theres a huge bell down there in the water what said dora she half rose amazed scarcely understanding him yes said toby pleased with the effect he had produced isn't it odd I found it when I was swimming underwater

18. Do the same with this extract from *The Canterville Ghost*, by Oscar Wilde:

Suddenly Mrs Otis caught sight of a dull red stain on the floor just by the fireplace and quite unconscious of what it really signified said to Mrs Umney I am afraid something has been spilt there yes madam replied the old housekeeper in a low voice blood has been spilt on that spot how horrid cried Mrs Otis I dont at all care for blood stains in a sitting room it must be removed at once the old woman smiled and answered in the same low mysterious voice it is the blood of Lady Eleanore de Canterville who was murdered on that very spot by her own husband Sir Simon de Canterville in 1575.

19. And with this lively passage from *The Wind in the Willows*, by Kenneth Grahame:

Aha that squeaky board in the butlers pantry said Toad now I understand it we shall creep out quietly into the butlers pantry cried the Mole with our pistols and swords and sticks shouted the Rat and rush in upon them said the Badger and whack em and whack em and whack em cried the Toad in ecstasy running round and round the room and jumping over the chairs

20. Here is an extract from a play – *John Bull's Other Island*, by George Bernard Shaw. Can you punctuate it and set it out as it would appear in the drama script? (N.B.

Inverted commas, or quotation marks, are not required in this exercise.)

DOYLE . . . hes not an Irishman at all BROADBENT not an Irishman he is so amazed by this statement that he straightens himself and brings the stool bolt upright DOYLE born in Glasgow never was in Ireland in his life I know all about him BROADBENT but he spoke he behaved just like an Irishman DOYLE like an Irishman is it possible that you dont know that all this top o the morning and broth of a boy and more power to your elbow business is as peculiar to England as the Albert Hall concerts of Irish music are no Irishman ever talks like that in Ireland or ever did or ever will

21. Punctuate and arrange in dramatic form this passage from John Osborne's play, *The Hotel in Amsterdam*:

MARGARET leave her alone there are some problems you've never had to face LAURIE I should hope so the telephone in the sitting room rings they stare at it who the devils that MARGARET well youd better answer it LAURIE she hasn't told anyone else where we are MARGARET no no one she hasn't spoken to anyone well pick it up ANNIE does so ANNIE room number whats this one three two O yes no just a moment its for Amy LAURIE Amy ANNIE Amy phone its for you they wait AMY appears putting on her dressing gown AMY for me how do they know LAURIE Ill tell you

22. Punctuate and arrange in verse lines this passage from Alexander Pope's poem, *An Essay on Man*:

Say first of God above or Man below what can we reason but from what we know of Man what see we but his station here from which to reason or to which refer thro worlds unnumbered tho the God be known tis ours to trace him only in our own

23. This short poem by Walter de la Mare consists of twelve irregular lines. Can you arrange and punctuate them?

What did you say I nothing no what was that sound when then I do not know whose eyes were those on us where there no eyes I saw speech footfall presence how cold the night may be phantom or fantasy its all one to me

24. Treat similarly this verse from Sir John Betjeman's poem, '*Christmas*':

And is it true and is it true this most tremendous tale of all seen in a stained glass windows hue a baby in an oxs stall the maker of the stars and sea become a child on earth for me

25. Here is an extract from a note (in 'The Writers' and Artists' Year Book') on the most valuable of all literary prizes. Punctuation marks and capital letters have been omitted. You are asked to supply them.

The nobel prize in literature is one of the awards stipulated in the will of the late alfred nobel the swedish scientist who invented dynamite . . . for authors writing in english it was bestowed upon rudyard kipling in 1907 upon w b yeats in 1923 upon george bernard shaw in 1925 upon sinclair lewis in 1930 upon john galsworthy in 1932 upon eugene o neill in 1936 upon pearl buck in 1938 upon t s eliot in 1948 upon william faulkner in 1949 upon bertrand russell in 1950 upon sir winston churchill in 1953 upon ernest hemingway in 1954 and upon John steinbeck in 1962

8

WHO WROTE WHAT?

'Language is a common heritage, and in proportion as we understand it at all its levels, literature becomes a common heritage also.' The writer here is a distinguished philologist, G. H. Vallins, author of some admirable books on the nature and practice of written English. In the third volume of his popular trilogy (*Good English, Better English* and *The Best English*), he also says: 'Literature, as distinct from ephemeral writing and officialese, preserves what is best and most worthy out of the past and hands it on as a living tradition; and since it has permanence, we are conscious of the continuity.'

Are we really as conscious as we claim to be of the wealth and continuity of what we proudly call our literary heritage? The questions in this section will help the reader to answer that question for himself. Their purpose is not to 'catch him out' but to remind him afresh of the long procession of good writers in whose works he may find all the elements of what is called 'Good English'.

1. A suggestion by Harry Bailey, mine host of the Tabard Inn, led to a memorable spate of story-telling. Can you explain? What name is given to the collected stories, and who wrote them?

2. He was born in Shropshire about 1330, but left the Malvern Hills to settle in London, in Cornhill, with his wife Kitte and his daughter Calote. A public scribe, he has left us an impression of himself as a tall, gaunt monkish

fellow (he had a shaven crown) who strode haughtily through the streets doing reverence to neither lords nor ladies. Many people took him for a madman.

Who was he? In what work did he speak of himself and his opinions on the life of his day?

3. 'Everyman, I will go with thee, and be thy guide,
In thy most need to go by thy side.'

The play *Everyman*, from which these lines are taken, is still occasionally acted, but it belongs to the earliest types of dramas in our literature, the religious or semi-religious plays popular in the fifteenth century, and probably even earlier. If we call these types the '3 M's', can you give the three names in full, and say to which type *Everyman* belongs?

4. The Renaissance may be said to have started in England with the writings of a learned lawyer who was honoured and, later, executed by his royal master, Henry VIII. His most famous book was founded on Plato's *Republic*, and is the story of an imaginary island whose people live ideally happy lives.

Who was he? What did he call his book?

5. (*a*) He called merry London 'my most kindly nurse'.
(*b*) He said 'the man who is tired of London is tired of life'.

Name these celebrated lovers of London.

6. He sold his soul to the Devil in return for twenty-four years of absolute power and self-indulgence.

Who did? Who created him?

7. 'This was the noblest Roman of them all . . .'

Who was? Who said so? In which play do we meet them?

8. Complete these titles of five of Shakespeare's plays:

(*a*) *Antony and* - - - - - - -

(*b*) *Timon of* - - - - - - -

(*c*) *Measure for* - - - - - - - -

(*d*) *Two Gentlemen of* - - - - - - -

(*e*) *Troilus and* - - - - - - - - -

9. This man, famous for his essays, was described by a later writer, Alexander Pope, as 'the greatest, wisest, meanest of mankind'.

Who was he? Explain the criticism.

One of his contemporaries was described as 'the wisest fool in Christendom'.

In what way were the two men connected?

10. An experiment in refrigeration is said to have cost the first of the two men his life. What happened?

11. A seventeenth-century poet wrote, after a period of imprisonment:

'Stone walls do not a prison make,
Nor iron bars a cage . . .'

Who was he? Why was he imprisoned? Can you quote the last two lines of the verse?

12. 'Eyeless in Gaza, at the mill with slaves . . .'

Who was? From what poem is this line taken? Who wrote it? Can you name the author of a modern novel with the title, *Eyeless in Gaza*?

13. He wrote *The Life and Death of Mr. Badman*, but his fame rests on another tale of a man who goes from a bad place to a better. Can you name: (*a*) the author, (*b*) the traveller, (*c*) the better book, (*d*) the two places, his home town and his destination?

14. What poet said of what king?

> 'He nothing common did or mean
> Upon that memorable scene . . .'

And what scene did he mean? Can you quote the last two lines of the quatrain?

15. 'He that complies against his will
    Is of the same opinion still.'

The author of these lines lived at the time of the Restoration. The long humorous poem for which he is best known is a satire in which he holds up to ridicule the habits of the Roundheads.

Name the author and the poem.

16. It was first published in 1825, one hundred and twenty-two years after its author's death. For most of that time, the manuscript, which was in shorthand, had remained unread in the Archives of Magdalene College, Cambridge.

What are we talking about?

17. Can you name the 17th-century diary writer who discovered the great wood carver, Grinling Gibbons, and brought his work to the notice of the King?

18. Who wrote *Annus Mirabilis*? What type of work is it? What does the title mean? What year is referred to and why is it so called?

19. A foppish young aristocrat who, in a party prank, snipped off a lock of a young lady's hair, provided a famous poet of the day with the theme of one of his most brilliant poems. Can you name . . .?

(*a*) the poet (*b*) the poem (*c*) the poet's name for the heroine.

20. One of Dean Swift's most powerful pamphlets was written as a virulent protest against a patent given by the English Government to a man named Wood to supply Ireland with half-pennies.

Name the pamphlet.

21. What one might call a breakfast-table problem was the cause of fierce party rivalry in one of the countries visited by the hero of Swift's *Gulliver's Travels*.

Explain, please.

22. Addison and Steele are best known as pioneer journalists. Can you say when they wrote, and name the two papers in which their essays appeared?

23. 'The first of our Society is a Gentleman from Worcestershire, of ancient Descent, a Baronet . . . His Great Grandfather was Inventor of that famous Country-Dance which is call'd after him.'

Can you name this eccentric baronet, introduced here by Steele in his first account of the fictitious Club?

24. The adventures of a shipwrecked sailor marooned on a desert island in 1714 gave an elderly fiction writer (he was nearly 60 when his book was published) the idea for his best-known story.

Name: (*a*) the author (*b*) the story (*c*) the real name of the sailor (*d*) the island.

Later, a well-known poem was written on the supposed meditations of the lonely mariner. Who wrote it? Can you quote the first two lines?

25. Sir Joshua Reynolds told of once seeing a famous poet at an auction of books or pictures. It was about the year 1740. He remembered that there was a lane formed to let the poet pass freely through the assemblage, and he proceeded along it bowing to those who were on each side. 'He was about four feet six high; very humpbacked and deformed; he wore a black coat; and according to the fashion of the time, had on a little sword.'

Have you recognised the poet? One of his poems is a satire on literary incompetence; he imagines a kingdom of ignoramuses in which the highest honours fall to the dullest of the critics and writers who were his enemies. What is it called?

26. Can you name a famous national song which appeared in a work called *The Masque of Alfred*, written jointly by James Thomson and David Mallet? The poet Southey called the song 'the political hymn of this country as long as she maintains her political power'.

Quote, if you can, the first verse and the chorus.

27. Who said: 'No man but a blockhead ever wrote except for money.'? (Incidentally, do you know how much John Milton was paid for *Paradise Lost*?)

28. 'He owes his place in the history of literature to his revolt against the artificial poetry established by Pope . . .'

Who does? He wrote *The Seasons* and *The Castle of Indolence*. In what ways do these poems differ from other poetical works of the period?

29. He lived to become the dominant literary figure of the 18th-century. Andrew Lang described him as 'One of the wisest, greatest, best, and most humorous of Englishmen.'

Of whom was he speaking? Can you answer these questions on the man and his work?

(*a*) As a child he was taken to London to be 'touched' by Queen Anne. Explain.

(*b*) At one time he set up a school in his native town of Lichfield, but had only three pupils. One of these, however, accompanied him to London and became the most famous actor of his time. Name him.

(*c*) His mother died in 1759. One of his books, a prose romance, was written in a single week to pay for her funeral. What was it called?

(*d*) He is sometimes referred to as 'the great lexicographer'. Why?

30. It was curfew time, and the author of one of the most popular poems in English literature was watching the cows coming home, and

'The ploughman homeward plods his weary way,
And leaves the world to darkness and to me', he said.

Who was he? Where was he? What did he call the poem inspired by his lonely vigil?

31. An urgent message called Dr. Johnson one morning to the lodgings of a friend, whom he found in some distress. His landlady had 'arrested' him (presumably by confiscating his trousers) for failing to pay his rent. Looking for some means of extricating him, Johnson found his friend had a novel ready for the press. He examined it and, seeing its merit, took it at once to a bookseller and sold it for £60.

Who was the impecunious friend? What book did Johnson sell for him?

32. In 1770 (the year when the great poet Wordsworth was born), a young unrecognised poet poisoned himself in a Holborn lodging-house. A precocious boy with an insatiable interest in the past, he had written in a medieval style some ballads and other verses which he published at Bristol in 1768. To attract attention to them, he pretended to have discovered manuscripts containing the work of a 15th-century monk. Literary critics who had seen merit in the poems turned against him when the hoax was exposed.

Who was 'the marvellous boy', as Wordsworth called him? What name did he give to the fictitious monk?

33. In the year 1786, a young failed farmer from Mossgiel near Mauchline decided to emigrate to Jamaica, where a post had been found for him. To pay for his passage, he brought out his first book of poems. Its success was so great that he gave up the idea of emigrating.

His name? He married Jean Armour, but he was fond of the ladies and wrote poems to more than one. Of which of them did he write:

> 'But to see her was to love her,
> Love but her, and love for ever'?

34. The novel as we know it to-day dates from 1741 when a Derbyshire-born printer published a romantic story about a servant girl pursued, with dark designs, by her employer's son.

Who was the author? (He held the office of Law Printer to the King.)

What was the novel called? (It has the sub-title, *or Virtue Rewarded.*) In what unusual form was the story presented?

35. A contemporary novelist was to win a far greater reputation as a literary craftsman and creator of character. His best novel appeared in 1749, and was the story of a foundling. A highly successful modern film was based on it. Can you name the book and the author? He did much good work in fighting crime in London. What public office did he hold?

36. Another 18th-century novelist and critic, Horace Walpole, sent a copy of his book to his friend, Thomas Gray, the poet. Gray replied: 'I have received the *Castle of Otranto* and return you my thanks for it. It engages our attention here, makes some of us cry a little, and all in general afraid to go to bed o' nights.'

What made Gray's family afraid to go to bed, and why is that book significant in the history of the English novel?

37. This poet wrote 'John Gilpin's Ride to York' and 'God moves in a mysterious way'. Who was he?

His well-known hymns appeared, together with those of his friend, the Rev. John Newton, in a collection named after the little town where he lived. What town was that?

38. From a century deficient in good drama, only a few comedies have survived and enjoyed a lasting popularity.

Goldsmith's *She Stoops to Conquer* was one of these. A fellow dramatist, also born in Ireland, wrote two others which are regarded as model comedies, distinguished for their polished dialogue and humorous situations. Unlike Goldsmith, he was at ease in society, a brilliant speaker who became a Member of Parliament for Stafford. He managed two of London's biggest theatres, until his lack of business ability and the destruction by fire of the Drury Lane Theatre left him impoverished and deserted by his former admirers.

Who was he? Name his two most successful plays.

39. During a walk over the Quantock Hills, two friends planned to produce a volume of poems which should express their dislike of the artificial poetic diction of the 18th-century. The book was published in 1798. Under what title? Can you name the poets and mention an outstanding poem by each?

40. 'Bliss was it in that - - - - - - to be alive,
But to be - - - - - - was very heaven.'

Fill in the missing words. To what event does the poet refer?

41. W - - - - - - - - -, C - - - - - - - - - - - and S - - - - - - - - - - - are often called the Lake Poets. Name them. Which two of them became in turn Poet Laureate?

42. Who said he woke up one morning and found himself famous? What had he done? In 1824, he joined the Greeks in their rebellion against Turkish oppression and gave ten thousand pounds to the cause.

How did he die?

43. The poet Coleridge described an encounter with one of his admirers: "A loose, slack, not well-dressed youth met Mr. Green and myself in a lane near Highgate. He was introduced to me and stayed a minute or so. After he had left us a little way, he came back and said: 'Let me carry away the memory of having pressed your hand.' – 'There is death in that hand,' I said when he had gone; yet this was, I believe, before the consumption showed itself distinctly."

Name the youth. What do you know of his death?

44. A stained-glass window in Winchester Cathedral is a memorial to one of the greatest of English novelists – a novelist who, in the opinion of Sir Walter Scott, had 'a talent for describing the involvements and feelings and characters of ordinary life which is to me the most wonderful I ever met with . . .'

Can you identify this superlative novelist and name three of the novels which drew such extravagant praise from Sir Walter's pen?

45. The poet Shelley was sent down from University College, Oxford, in 1811. Do you know why? He also died young, at the age of thirty. Say what you know of the circumstances of his death.

46. 'Earth has not anything to show more fair . . .'

Than what? Who said it? Where was he standing at the time?

47. In April 1821, John Murray, the publisher, received a letter from one of his authors, who asked: 'Is it true, what Shelley writes me, that poor John Keats died at Rome of the *Quarterly Review*? I am very sorry for it . . . I know,

by experience, that a savage review is Hemlock to a sucking author; and the one on me knocked me down – but I got up again.'

Who wrote that letter? He referred to the subject later in a satirical verse:

> 'Who killed John Keats?
> 'I,' said the *Quarterly*,
> Savage and tartarly,
> 'Twas one of my feats.'

What was all the fuss about? This poet had his revenge for the attack on himself in another satirical work. What was it called?

48. Shelley, writing to his friend Joseph Severn, said:

'I send you the elegy on poor Keats – and I wish it were better worth your acceptance.'

Can you name the elegy? Quote any well-known lines from it. Two other famous elegies are *Lycidas* and *In Memoriam*. Who wrote them? On whom?

49. Here is an extract from a letter written by Sir Walter Scott to his son-in-law, J. G. Lockhart:

'I have had visits from all the monied people, offering their purses – and those who are creditors sending their managers to assure me of their joining in and adopting any measures I may propose . . . A penny I will not borrow from anyone. Since my creditors are content to be patient, I have the means of righting them perfectly . . .'

What had happened? How did Scott try to put things right?

50. A hundred years after the time of Addison and Steele, the essay as introduced by them enjoyed a new period of popularity. One of the best-loved essayists spent most of his working life at a desk in the East India House. Though

he rejoiced at being 'a freed man after thirty-three years' slavery', he had a domestic tragedy which clouded his life, compelling him to devote most of his time to the care of his sister. She, too, was a gifted writer, but mentally unstable and liable to frenzied outbursts.

Who was the essayist? How did his sister's mental state bring tragedy to their home? She collaborated with her brother in a successful book of stories. What were they called? What title did the brother give to his own book of essays?

51. Another early 19th-century essayist was a drug addict who ran away from his home near Manchester and led a vagabond life in London. At one time, he was befriended by a London prostitute. Who was he? In what book did he tell the unfortunate girl's story? Later, having returned to his family, he went to Oxford and made literature his profession. Having made the acquaintance of three other writers, a well-known trio of poets, he made his home for the next twenty years in the district made popular by them. Where was it?

52. Of which poet did a cynical critic remark that 'after filling the world with his verse he was now emptying the Globe with his prose.'? To what prose works did the critic refer? A contemporary prose writer has described the poet as he saw him: 'One of the finest looking men in the world. A great shock of rough dusky dark hair; bright, laughing, hazel eyes; massive aquiline face, most massive yet most delicate; of sallow brown complexion, almost Indian looking, clothes cynically loose. Free-and-easy, smokes infinite tobacco. His voice is musical, metallic, fit for loud laughter and piercing wail, and all that may lie between . . .'

Whose words are these? What high honour had been bestowed upon the poet he was describing?

53. The philosophy of this poet is perhaps best expressed in his own words: 'God's in his Heaven – All's right with the world.' With unquenchable optimism, he wooed and won and eloped with a sickly poetess, much to the displeasure of her stern father. You know his name, of course. Can you also say . . . ?

(*a*) in what poem do the lines quoted above appear?

(*b*) who is the lost leader in his poem under that title?

(*c*) from where to where did they bring 'the good news' in another of his well known poems?

(*d*) what was the name of his wife, and for what poems is she remembered?

54. Another Victorian poet who married a sick wife had a less happy marriage. Overcome with grief, and perhaps remorse, at her early death from an overdose of laudanum, he put the manuscript of his poems in her coffin to be buried with her. Can you name him? (The poems were retrieved later and published.)

He was also a painter of considerable ability. With Holman Hunt, Millais and other artists, he formed an aesthetic Brotherhood which had a peculiar influence on the art and literature of the period. What name was given to it?

55. 'The last great Englishman is low' sang Tennyson in an elegiac ode written in 1852. Whose death was he mourning?

56. The fame of this poet rests entirely on one poem, a translation of the work of a Persian poet-astronomer of the eleventh century, which he had discovered when visiting the Bodleian Library in Oxford, in 1856. As no publisher would print the poem, he had copies (two hundred and fifty) printed at his own expense. Even then, there was no demand for them until the poet Rossetti came upon a

copy and, deeply moved by it, recommended the poem to his friends.

Give the title of the translation and the name of the translator.

57. The novels of Charles Dickens are crowded with characters whose names have become household words.

Can you answer these questions on his life and works?

(*a*) In which town, a seaport, was he born?

(*b*) What was the family's connection with the Debtors' Prison of the Marshalsea?

(*c*) Where did the boy work when compelled to earn his own living, and how much did he earn?

(*d*) In what skill did he become proficient when he became a journalist?

(*e*) Of what newspaper did he become the first editor in 1846?

(*f*) Ten years earlier, his first book of 'sketches' had appeared. Under what title?

(*g*) A firm of publishers (Chapman and Hall) wanted a story to illustrate the drawings of a popular artist and invited Dickens to write it. What was the result?

(*h*) Which of his novels deal with (i) the French Revolution, and (ii) the Gordon Riots?

(*i*) When famous, he toured Great Britain and America. Doing what?

(*j*) In which novels do we find? – Sarah Gamp, Sam Weller, Mr. Bumble, Mr. Micawber, Sydney Carton.

58. A Victorian novelist whose life span covered almost the same years as that of Dickens also gave lectures in this country and in America. He lectured on *The Four Georges* and *English Humourists of the 18th Century*. Like Dickens, he began his writing with sketches, with *The Paris Sketch Book* and *Comic Talks and Sketches*. He wrote for *Punch*,

and his *Snob Papers* (later called *The Book of Snobs*) had considerable success.

Who was he? If you have not recognised him from the information given, it may help to be reminded that he was the creator of such vividly depicted characters as Becky Sharp, Rawdon Crawley and Henry Esmond.

Name the works in which they appear. With what period of English history does the story of Esmond deal?

59. Another novelist of Victorian times was a statesman and became Prime Minister. He once described a political rival as 'a sophistical rhetorician, inebriated with the exuberance of his own verbosity.'

Name the two men and, if you can, say when this was said. Mention two novels written by the statesman.

60. 'Her countenance was equine – she was rather like a horse; and her head had been intended for a much longer body – she was not a tall woman. She wore her hair in not pleasing, out-of-fashion loops, coming down on either side of her face, so hiding her ears; and her garments concealed her outline – they gave her a waist like a milestone.'

This is Frederick Locker-Lampson's unflattering portrait of one of the great women novelists of the nineteenth century. Can you recognise her? Her maiden name was as homespun and commonplace as her features, and she chose an unromantic masculine name for her pseudonym.

(Give both names.) There was, however, nothing commonplace in her writings; she ranks high among the greatest novelists in English Literature, as a shrewd and subtle observer of life and character.

One of her unforgettable characters is Mrs. Poyser, that waspish critic of the neighbours. In what novel does she appear? Can you name the devout Methodist preacher, a woman, in that book? Say also which of this novelist's stories deal with (*a*) the Renaissance in Italy, (*b*) a miser, reformed by affection for an abandoned baby.

61. The story of the three Brontë sisters has often been told. Their lives were tragically brief, but their works have ensured them permanent niches in literature's hall of fame. They have been called the most famous example of group or family genius in England. They wrote poems as well as novels, and like the Lake Poets they have become permanently linked with a particular part of the country. Which part?

Of which parish church was their father incumbent? Name the three sisters, and the brother who was the cause of great anxiety to the family. What was his trouble? Which sister married her father's former curate and died in childbirth? And which wrote which of the following novels?

Shirley, Wuthering Heights, Villette, Wildfell Hall, Jane Eyre.

62. Here are the titles of famous novels written by other nineteenth century authors:

Westward Ho! *Lavengro* *The Cloister and the Hearth*
Cranford *Barchester Towers* *The Moonstone*

Select the authors from this group:—

Charles Reade Wilkie Collins Elizabeth Gaskell
George Borrow Anthony Trollope Charles Kingsley

63. This author is a 'regional' novelist. He wrote the *Wessex Tales*. Can you give his name? Which counties provide the settings for most of his stories? Supply the missing words in these titles of some of his novels:

(*a*) Far from the . . . .

(*b*) Under the . . . .

(*c*) The Return of . . . .

(*d*) Tess of . . . .

(*e*) Jude the . . . .

He is usually regarded as a pessimist, portraying his characters as the puppets of fate. He is said to have given up novel writing after the unfavourable reception of one of his books. Which book? He turned then to poetry, and also wrote a chronicle play on Wessex during the Napoleonic wars. What was its title?

64. Can you name the author of each of these children's 'classics'?

(*a*) *The Wind in the Willows*

(*b*) *Peter Pan*

(*c*) *Alice in Wonderland*

(*d*) *The Jungle Book*

(*e*) *Black Beauty*

(*f*) *Tom Brown's Schooldays*

(*g*) *Treasure Island*

As they are not given here in chronological order, can you select the correct date for each from the following list? 1857, 1865, 1877, 1883, 1894, 1904, 1908.

Which of the stories was written by a woman? Which was written in the form of a play? Which are animal stories? For which of them did the author use a pen name?

65. Who wrote *The Importance of Being Earnest*? What kind of work is it? The author served a term of imprisonment and subsequently wrote a long poem based on his experiences. What did he call the poem?

66. In which long narrative poem do we read of a drunken prize-fighter who is reformed through the influence of a Quaker woman mission worker? Do you know the man's name? Who wrote the poem? He had been a seaman and his knowledge and love of the sea was reflected in such well known poems as *Cargoes* and *Sea Fever*. He was made Poet Laureate in 1930.

67. His name was Korzeniowski; he was a Pole born in the Ukraine, and knew no English until he became a seaman in the British Merchant Service. Under what name did he become famous as a writer of the best English fiction of his time? His first book was *Almayer's Folly*, published in 1895, the story of an eastern river. He died in 1924.

Complete these titles of some of his novels:—

An Outcast of the I........

The Arrow of G......

Under Western E.......

The Secret A.......

The Nigger of the N.......

68. Some of the stories written by this novelist are notable for their co-ordination of science and fiction, anticipating 'Dr. Who' and other heroes of the space age. He wrote *The Time Machine* and *The Invisible Man*. After a grammar school education, he began working at thirteen as a salesman in drapers' establishments. Later, he became a teacher, won a scholarship to the Royal College of Science, and graduated with first-class honours. He died in 1946.

Who was he? In which book did he anticipate in fiction the lunar landings of our time?

Complete these titles of other novels by him:—

Love and Mr. L........

The Island of Dr. M......

The World of William C.......

The History of Mr. P........

Mr. B...... Sees it Through

69. With the publication of *The Old Wives' Tale* in 1908, this author established himself as a master of modern fiction. He was already known as a regional novelist, with *Anna of the Five Towns* and other stories of 'The Potteries', where he was born. Can you name the Five Towns? He

was an immensely successful novelist and playwright, and was not ashamed to admit that he wrote for money. Who was he? His first Christian name was Enoch, but he appears to have been a little ashamed of that and did not use it on his books. Can you complete these titles?

The Grand . . . . . . Hotel

Imperial . . . .

Riceyman . . . .

70. Another popular novelist and playright, J. B. Priestley, has experimented in many literary fields. In addition to novels and plays, he has written travel books, essays, and critical studies on *English Humour*, *The English Novel* and *Figures in Modern Literature*.

Can you give the titles of: (*a*) his best-selling novel, published in 1929, and (*b*) two plays in which he experimented with a new time theory?

71. Here is a pen portrait of a great twentieth-century novelist as a fellow writer saw him at their first and only meeting. Sir Osbert Sitwell, invited to have tea with the novelist, was accompanied by his sister Edith, the poet. They found their host living in a farmhouse in Tuscany: 'He opened the door to us, and it was the first time I had ever realised what a fragile and goatish little saint he was: a Pan and a Messiah: for in his flattish face, with its hollow, wan cheeks, and rather red beard, was to be discerned a curious but happy mingling of satyr and ascetic . . .'

Do you recognise him? He was poet and painter as well as novelist. He had eloped with the German wife of a distinguished English professor of languages, and they were living abroad, moving from place to place, presumably in search of the sun for he was already a sick man. (He died in 1930 at the age of 45.) Of his upbringing, a contemporary novelist and poet, Richard Church, has said: 'Born in 1885, he was reared during the ugliest period of

English culture, in the ugliest part of England.' Where was that? What was his father's occupation?

Can you give . . . ? (*a*) the title of his first novel; (*b*) the title of the autobiographical novel which made him famous; (*c*) the title of a supposedly obscene novel, formerly banned and later the cause of a celebrated court action.

72. A once-banned novel of far greater significance in contemporary fiction was written by the Irish author James Joyce. On its appearance in 1922, it was suppressed in Great Britain and in the United States; but its importance as a unique work of genius is now universally recognised. It has been called the mastodon of contemporary fiction, the total effect of which is 'one of unparalleled stylistic brilliance, of the most complex cultural intellectuality'.

What is it called? Who is the hero or central character?

How much of his life is covered by the events described or reflected on?

Ten years earlier, the author wrote a book of short stories. What did he call that? It was followed in 1916 by an autobiographical work in which the author revealed 'an almost dismaying power to exploit the religious and sexual consciousness of adolescence'. Can you name it?

73. Here are ten representative novels by other well known authors of this century. Can you assign them to the correct authors, whose names you will find in the list below?

(*a*) *The Man of Property*
(*b*) *Of Human Bondage*
(*c*) *Kim*
(*d*) *A Passage to India*
(*e*) *To the Lighthouse*
(*f*) *Decline and Fall*
(*g*) *Brave New World*
(*h*) *The Power and the Glory*
(*i*) *Nineteen Eighty-Four*
(*j*) *Lucky Jim*

(Graham Greene, Somerset Maugham, Evelyn Waugh, Kingsley Amis, E. M. Forster, Rudyard Kipling, Aldous Huxley, Virginia Woolf, George Orwell, John Galsworthy)

74. Which poet wrote a sonnet beginning . . . ?

'Now, God be thanked Who has matched us with His hour . . .'

What hour was he thinking of? Unfortunately, he himself did not survive the hour of testing. How and where did he die?

75. 'I will arise and go now,
      And go to . . . . . '

Where? Who said he was going? And what did he propose to do when he got there?

76. A dominant influence on the poetry of the last half century has been the work of the poet and critic T. S. Eliot. His most significant and influential poem was published in 1922 (the year of *Ulysses*, which gave a new dimension to the novel). What did he call it? It was followed by four poems whose titles (according to Richard Church) became more and more arid and lava-like: *Ash Wednesday*, *East Coker*, *Burnt Norton*, and *Dry Salvages*.

Two of Eliot's religious poems have been more popular, because easier to understand. Perhaps you can supply the missing words in their titles: *A Song for S. . . . . .*, and *Journey of the M . . . . . .*

He was also the author of a successful verse play on the subject of the death of the Archbishop Thomas à Becket. Can you name it?

77. T. S. Eliot was an American who came to England to complete his education and make his name. The dramatic scene in the first half of the twentieth century was dominated by an Irishman, George Bernard Shaw, who came over to teach the English how to write and speak their own language.

Can you answer these questions on his life and work?

(*a*) What kind of literary work did he engage in before writing plays?

(*b*) In which play did he deal with the political problems of his own country?

(*c*) The successful musical comedy *My Fair Lady* was based on one of Shaw's plays, in which a professor of phonetics undertakes the task of teaching a Cockney flower girl how to speak in immaculate English.

Give the title of the play and the names of the professor and the girl. A certain expression used by the girl is said to have startled the first-night audience when the play was produced. What did she say?

(*d*) In which of Shaw's plays is the heroine a Salvation Army officer?

(*e*) Which play touches on the persecution of the early Christians?

(*f*) What coveted award did Shaw receive in 1925?

(*g*) In what year did he die, and how old was he?

78. Find the authors of these representative twentieth-century plays, selecting from the names in the appended list:

Dear Brutus *Abraham Lincoln* *Juno and the Paycock* *Hay Fever* *Tobias and the Angel* *Waiting for Godot* *Under Milk Wood* *Look Back in Anger* *The Dumb Waiter* *A Man for All Seasons*

(John Osborne, Samuel Beckett, Sir James Barrie, Dylan Thomas, Harold Pinter, James Bridie, Robert Bolt, Sean O'Casey, John Drinkwater, Noel Coward.)

79. Can you name the writers of the following auto-biographical works?

(*a*) The autobiography of a Super-Tramp

(*b*) Far Away and Long Ago (*c*) The Summing-Up

(*d*) The Way of All Flesh

(*e*) The Story of My Heart

You will find the authors here:

W. Somerset Maugham William Henry Hudson
Richard Jefferies W. H. Davies
Samuel Butler

80. The titles of these contemporary works have become well known to the general public of film and television viewers. Can you say who wrote them?

(*a*) Lord of the Flies

(*b*) A Taste of Honey

(*c*) Cider with Rosie

(*d*) Room at the Top

(*e*) The Loneliness of the Long- Distance Runner

9

CAN YOU PLACE THEM ?

(A 'Quiz Quicky' Revision Test on Books and Authors)

Name the authors of these works:

1. (*a*) The Good Earth (*b*) The Good Companions (*c*) Good Wives (*d*) The Good-Natured Man

2. (*a*) The Village (*b*) Our Village (*c*) The Village Minstrel (*d*) The Deserted Village

3. (*a*) Father and Son (*b*) Sons and Lovers (*c*) Dombey and Son

4. (*a*) Northanger Abbey (*b*) South Riding (*c*) East Lynne (*d*) Westward Ho!

5. (*a*) The Golden Age (*b*) The Golden Bowl (*c*) The Golden Bough

6. (*a*) Utopia (*b*) A Modern Utopia (*c*) Erewhon (*d*) The New Atlantis

Name the authors of these works:

7. (*a*) Lord Jim (*b*) Lucky Jim

8. (*a*) Old Mortality (*b*) Old St. Paul's
(*c*) The Old Wives' Tale (*d*) The Old Curiosity Shop

9. (*a*) New Grub Street (*b*) A New Way to Pay Old Debts
(*c*) The New Arabian Nights

10. (*a*) The White Company (*b*) The White Monkey
(*c*) White Fang (*d*) The White Peacock
(*e*) The White Devil (*f*) The Woman in White

11. (*a*) The Black Arrow (*b*) The Black Dwarf
(*c*) The Black Tulip (*d*) Black Beauty

12. (*a*) The Last Days of Pompeii
(*b*) The Last of the Barons
(*c*) The Last of the Mohicans
(*d*) The Last Chronicle of Barset

13. (*a*) A Song of David (*b*) A Song for Simeon
(*c*) Absalom and Achitophel (*d*) Samson Agonistes

14. (*a*) Ash Wednesday (*b*) Good Friday
(*c*) The Man Who was Thursday
(*d*) Saturday Night and Sunday Morning

15. (*a*) The Open Road (*b*) The Dover Road
(*c*) Sinister Street (*d*) The Broad Highway
(*e*) The Path to Rome

Name the authors of these works:

16. (*a*) Emma (*b*) Pamela (*c*) Sybil
(*d*) Trilby (*e*) Vanessa

17. Here are the names of some well-known literary pets:
(*a*) Dinah (*b*) Flush (*c*) Boatswain
(*d*) Hodge (*e*) Selima

Can you say:

To whom they belonged?
What they were – e.g. cats or dogs?
Which were real and which fictitious?

18. Which is the 'odd man out' in each of these groups?
(*a*) Byron Tennyson Dickens Bacon Macaulay
(*b*) Sir Walter Raleigh Sir Richard Steele
Sir John Betjeman Sir Roger de Coverley
Sir James Barrie

19. In which of Charles Dickens' novels do we meet:
(*a*) The Fat Boy (*b*) Pip (*c*) Tiny Tim
(*d*) Little Nell (*e*) The Artful Dodger

20. Who wrote under the following pen names?
Acton Bell John Sinjohn Lewis Carroll
Mark Twain George Orwell

21. Can you say where the action takes place in these 'regional' novels?
(*a*) *Sons and Lovers* (*b*) *Lorna Doone*
(*c*) *Rogue Herries* (*d*) *Wuthering Heights*
(*e*) *Far From the Madding Crowd*

22. Give the Christian names of these authors:

W. H. Auden　G. K. Chesterton　T. S. Eliot
W. W. Jacobs　J. B. Priestley　H. G. Wells

23. Each of these writers is usually paired with another. Can you supply the missing name?

Addison and ....　Beaumont and ....
Wordsworth and .....　Boswell and ....
Wyatt and ....

24. Say which of the works in each of these groups is the odd one out:

(*a*) *The Awkward Age. Daisy Miller. Guy Mannering. The Ambassadors*
(*b*) *Barry Lyndon. Catriona. Weir of Hermiston. Kidnapped*
(*c*) *Hypatia. Our Mutual Friend. Yeast. The Water Babies*

25. Who wrote these travel books?

(*a*) *Innocents Abroad*　(*b*) *Sea and Sardinia*
(*c*) *The Bible in Spain*　(*d*) *Rural Rides*
(*e*) *Travels with a Donkey in the Cevennes*

You will find the authors' names here, though not in the right order:

D. H. Lawrence　William Cobbett
R. L. Stevenson　George Borrow
Mark Twain

Part Two
ANSWERS

I

HOW DID IT START?

1\. *Old English*
Worth (farm)
Combe (a hollow)
Ham (home)
Field (Clearing)
Stan (stone)

Danish
Ness (headland)
Gate (a way)
Ford (estuary)
Holm (river flat)
Toft (farm)

Celtic
Aber (river mouth)
Avon (water)
Ex (water)
Llan (church)
Inver (river mouth)

Latin
Cester (camp)
Strata (paved road)
Port (harbour)
Fos(*sa*)-(ditch)
Coln (colony)

2\. *410.* Romans leave Britain. End of first Latin period.
597. Introduction of Christianity by Augustine.
1066. Norman invasion. Latin and French become languages of Church and State.
1453. Capture of Constantinople by the Turks. End of Eastern Roman Empire and beginning of the Renaissance (or Renascence), a re-birth of interest in the Greek and Latin classics.

3\. *1258.* Parliament proclaimed in English.
1348. English first taught in schools.
1362. English used in Law Courts.
1477. Printing introduced into England by Caxton.
1611. Authorised Version of the Bible issued.

4. (*a*) *altus* – high (*b*) *dominus* – lord (*c*) *fides* – faith (*d*) *liber* – free (*e*) *manus* – hand

5. (*a*) *porta* – gate (*b*) *sacer* – sacred (*c*) *umbra* – shade (*d*) *unda* – wave (*e*) *via* – a way

6. *centum* – hundred e.g. century, centipede
dictum – say e.g. dictate, verdict
erratum – wander e.g. erratic, error
flexum – bend e.g. deflect, flexible
gradus – a step e.g. gradient, degrade
cantum – sing e.g. cantata, incantation
corpus – body e.g. corporal, corpse
annus – year e.g. anniversary, annual
homo – man e.g. homicide, human
lectum – read e.g. lectern, lecture

7. *Latin*: alibi benefit brevity capital doctor
Greek: acrobat astrology autograph bible epigram

8. *anthos* (a flower) *derma* (skin) *logos* (word, speech) *khronos* (time) *mikros* (small)

9. *lithos* – a stone e.g. monolith, lithograph
pathos – suffering e.g. pathetic, sympathy
kuklos – circle e.g. bicycle, cyclone
oxus – sharp e.g. oxygen, paroxysm
isos – equal e.g. isosceles, isobar
klimax – ladder e.g. anticlimax, climacteric
phone – voice e.g. gramophone, euphony
theos – God e.g. atheist, theology
demos – people e.g. demagogue, democracy
metron – a measure e.g. symmetry, barometer

10. antic – antique amiable – amicable gentle – genteel
royal – regal secure – sure

11. chess (Persian) banana (Spanish) giraffe (African)
souvenir (French) typhoon (Chinese) waltz (German)
alcohol (Arabic) oasis (Egyptian) balcony (Italian)
marmalade (Portuguese)

12. moccasin (North American) stucco (Italian)
bungalow (Hindustani) garage (French)
chocolate (Mexican) sabbath (Hebrew)
paper (Egyptian) yacht (Dutch)
husband (Danish) chimpanzee (African)

13. canter { cypress, bayonet { damson,
port (wine) { copper tangerine { damask
milliner bunkum spaniel

14. (*a*) Atlas – Titan god whose shoulders held up the universe
Ceres – goddess of corn
Jove – Jove's planet believed to cause good humour
Bacchus – Greek god of wine
Fauna – sister of Latin god Faunus (the Greek god Pan)
Hector – Trojan hero of Homer's *Iliad*
Hygeia – Greek goddess of health
Mentor – adviser of Telemachus, son of Ulysses
Pan – Greek god reputed to cause panic among shepherds
Mercury – whose planet made those born under its influence light-hearted and vivacious

(*b*) Mars – god of war
Proteus – sea-god able to assume various shapes
Saturn – Roman god of agriculture, whose planet said by astrologers to produce a cold, gloomy temperament in people born under its influence
Vesta – goddess of the hearth in Roman mythology
Titans – Greek gods, children of Uranus, a gigantic race of superhuman size and strength
Vulcan – god of fire (volcanic and vulcanite from this name)
Hermes – god of secrets
Tantalus – condemned, in Greek mythology, to stand up to chin in water which receded when he tried to drink
Stentor – herald in Trojan War (Homer's *Iliad*)

15. (*a*) Tiw (Old English war god)
Woden (or Odin)
Thor (god of thunder)
Frig (wife of Odin)
Saturn (god of agriculture)

(*b*) Janus (Italian god, guardian of doors and gates)
Mars (god of war)
Julius Caesar
Augustus Caesar

16. Babel – the tower in Shinar (*Genesis*, xi)
Bedlam – hospital of St. Mary of Bethlehem used as a lunatic asylum
Jeremiah – the gloomy prophet
Lazarus – lazaretto a hospital for diseased poor, especially lepers (*St. Luke*, xvi, 20)
Magdalen(e) – the reformed prostitute identified with the sinner in *St. Luke*, vii, 37

17. brougham – a closed carriage, one-horse or electric (Lord Brougham – pron. *Broom*)
cardigan – a woollen over-waistcoat (Earl of Cardigan)
chesterfield – 1. type of couch; 2. kind of overcoat (Earl of Chesterfield)
petersham – 1. corded silk ribbon; 2. overcoat or breeches (Viscount Petersham)
sandwich – slices of bread with meat, etc. between them (prob. Earl of Sandwich)

18. bakelite – substitute for celluloid
galvanise – stimulation by shock or excitement
guillotine – instrument of execution (French)
hansom – a type of cab
mackintosh – waterproof material
pasteurise – to sterilise milk, etc.
daguerreotype – an early process in photography
silhouette – an outline portrait in profile
macadamise – to make roads with layers of broken stone
saxophone – musical instrument

19. (*a*) *derrick* – gallows, or crane with adjustable arm
(*b*) *burke* – to smother, suppress (Wm. Burke, executed 1829)
(*c*) *boycott* – cut off from social relations (Captain Charles Boycott, Irish land agent, ostracised by tenants, 1880–81)
(*d*) *zeppelin* – airship invented by Count Zeppelin
(*e*) *quisling* – traitor, from Quisling, Norwegian who collaborated with Nazis

20. *G. J. Kamel*, Jesuit botanist, in whose honour the camellia was named by Litannaeus (introduced to England, c. 1739)
Dahl, Swedish botanist, 1791

Leonard Fuchs, 16th-century German botanist

Sir W. Gage (c. 1725) who first introduced the fruit to England

Godet, Swiss botanist

M. de Lobel, Flemish naturalist (d. 1616)

P. Magnol, French botanist (d. 1715)

Logan, who obtained the fruit by crossing raspberry and blackberry

Eschscholtz, explorer

J. G. Zinn, German botanist

21. *arras* – rich tapestry, first made at Arras, town in Artois

calico – linen cloth, from Calicut, on Malabar coast, India

cambric – linen fabric, from Cambray, in France

diaper – linen fabric, associated with Ypres, in Belgium (but derived from Greek *aspros* –white)

gingham – cloth, probably from Guingamp, in Brittany

melton – kind of cloth, from Melton Mowbray, Leicestershire

muslin – fabric, from Mosul, town on the Tigris in Mesopotamia

nankeen – fabric, from Nanking, in China

tweed – cloth, from Tweed, the river, through confusion with 'twill', woven cloth

worsted – woollen yarn, from Worstead, in Norfolk

22. (*a*) trilby (*b*) martinet (*c*) mausoleum
(*d*) mesmerism (*e*) shrapnel (*f*) spoonerism
(*g*) silhouette (*h*) magenta (*i*) limerick
(*j*) palace

23. A patronymic is a name that indicates a son's (or daughter's) relationship to the father.

Robin*son* – son of Robin (English patronymic)
*P*ritchard – is the shortened form of the Welsh *ap Richard*, son of Richard
*Mac*donald – son of Donald (Scottish)
*Fitz*herbert – son of Herbert; the Norman prefix *Fitz* derived from the French *fils*
*O'*Donnell – son of Donnell (Irish)

24. *Vogue words* – certain words which have become 'fashionable' (and overworked) at various periods of the language.

(*a*) *appeasement* – used (since Neville Chamberlain's visit to Hitler) to express a policy of placating, or coming to terms with, aggressive dictators
(*b*) *blueprint* – post-war term for any re-building or re-planning scheme
(*c*) *liquidate* – euphemism used by the dictators to show their determination to wipe out all opponents
(*d*) *sanctions* – short for *punitive sanction*, as applied by United Nations (and League of Nations) to trade, etc., with offending countries – e.g. Rhodesia
(*e*) *totalitarian* – complete domination by the state, exacting obedience to authority, allowing no rivals – the policy of the Axis powers at the time of the Second World War

25. (*a*) to have a wash – hands and face
(*b*) the table at any special meal
(*c*) the poorer paid workers
(*d*) flowers at a funeral
(*e*) applied to meetings of heads of states or chief officials

2

WHAT'S THE WORD ?

1. (*a*) cosmopolitan (*b*) longevity (*c*) decorum
(*d*) laudable (*e*) vogue (*f*) robust
(*g*) steep (*h*) pulverise (*i*) cruciform
(*j*) serrated

2. (*a*) partition (*b*) petrify (*c*) immaculate
(*d*) surreptitious (*e*) ephemeral (*f*) sacrilege
(*g*) obliterate (*h*) pyrotechnics (*i*) colloquial
(*j*) perjury

3. (*a*) impalpable (*b*) inevitable (*c*) invulnerable
(*d*) indelible (*e*) insatiable (*f*) impregnable
(*g*) intangible (*h*) incomprehensible (*i*) invisible
(*j*) inaudible

4. (*a*) annuity (*b*) lectern (*c*) plagiarism
(*d*) affidavit (*e*) memorandum (*f*) emetic
(*g*) ruminant (*h*) factotum (*i*) proxy, or deputy
(*j*) anagram

5. (*a*) decapitate (*b*) exonerate (*c*) amnesty
(*d*) paragon (*e*) regicide (*f*) orthodox
(*g*) optical (*h*) oratory (*i*) capitulate
(*j*) reconnoitre

6. (*a*) anthropology (*b*) archaeology (*c*) biology
(*d*) entomology (*e*) ornithology (*f*) ethnology
(*g*) psychology (*h*) graphology (*i*) campanology
(*j*) technology

7. (*a*) biography (*b*) choreography (*c*) cartography
(*d*) geography (*e*) lithography (*f*) seismography
(*g*) hagiography (*h*) topography (*i*) bibliography
(*j*) photography

8. (*a*) accompanist (*b*) botanist (*c*) chiropodist
(*d*) dramatist (*e*) journalist (*f*) numismatist
(*g*) oculist (*h*) philatelist (*i*) taxidermist
(*j*) economist

9. (*a*) aristocracy (*b*) autocracy (*c*) bureaucracy
(*d*) democracy (*e*) plutocracy

10. (*a*) bishops, magistrates (*b*) directors, governors
(*c*) cardinals (*d*) jurymen
(*e*) police

11. (*a*) herd (*b*) flock (*c*) litter
(*d*) pack (*e*) nest

12. (*a*) bevy (*b*) building, or rookery
(*c*) covey (*d*) gaggle

13. (*a*) lapwings (*b*) peacocks
(*c*) pheasants (*d*) snipe

14. (*a*) cast – of hawks, actors
caste – of people in the social scale
(*b*) *troop* – of horsemen, or soldiers, antelopes, monkeys
troupe – of dancers, actors, acrobats, etc.

15. (*a*) down (*b*) cete (*c*) kindle (*d*) lepe (*e*) pace

16. (*a*) a pride of lions (*b*) a school of whales
(*c*) a skulk of foxes (*d*) a sounder of hogs
(*e*) a sleuth of bears

17. shoal of herrings horde of savages stud of horses
herd of buffaloes nest of beakers batch of bread
bunch of grapes chest of drawers clutch of eggs
flight of steps

18. library of books fell of hair swarm of bees
galaxy of stars skein of thread fleet of ships
stand of plovers watch of nightingales clump of trees
siege (or sedge) of herons

19. (*a*) arid (*b*) candid (*c*) frigid (*d*) lucid, limpid
(*e*) morbid (*f*) putrid (*g*) rapid (*h*) rancid
(*i*) turbid (*j*) insipid

20. (*a*) adumbrate (*b*) castigate (*c*) denigrate
(*d*) eradicate (*e*) fulminate (*f*) hibernate
(*g*) illustrate (*h*) litigate (*i*) nominate
(*j*) terminate

21. (*a*) accumulate (*b*) coagulate (*c*) disseminate
(*d*) emancipate (*e*) gyrate (*f*) lubricate
(*g*) modulate (*h*) promulgate (*i*) renovate
(*j*) vacillate

22. (*a*) aptitude (*b*) beatitude (*c*) decrepitude
(*d*) gratitude (*e*) ineptitude (*f*) latitude
(*g*) platitude (*h*) quietude (*i*) solicitude
(*j*) vicissitude

23. unofficial indefinite illiterate uncommon abnormal discourteous immoral illegible irresolute impossible indelicate ignoble impenitent disarrange unfashionable inapplicable immortal irreverent unveil nonsense

24. arduous–laborious
chagrin–vexation
emolument–profit
germane–relevant
fortuitous-accidental
latent–dormant
noisome-offensive
peccant–erring
repletion–satiety
temerity–rashness
bucolic–pastoral
dissolute–licentious
jocund–merry
immanent–inherent
hypothetical–conjectural
mercurial–volatile
opprobrium–disgrace
quandary–dilemma
succinct–terse
vituperate–revile

25. anomalous–regular
clandestine–manifest
fecundity–sterility
impecunious–affluent
hilarity–melancholy
opaque–transparent
reconcile–estrange
solitary–gregarious
deleterious–beneficial
nonchalant–excited
brusque–effusive
zeal–apathy
garrulous–taciturn
equity–injustice
malodorous–fragrant
permanent–temporary
theoretical–practical
winsome–unattractive
lugubrious–cheerful
veracious–false

26. advantageous burglarious comparative disciplinary
essential fraudulent glassy humorous
instrumental jocular knightly lay
mettlesome nosy oracular parochial
qualmish remedial splenetic titular (titled)
utilitarian vandalistic worshipful yeasty
zonal

27. manager manciple mandarin mannequin manikin

28. diploma dipper diplomat dipsomania diptych

29. pandemonium panegyric panjandrum panorama pantechnicon

30. funnel funereal fundamental fungicide functionary

31. furbish furbelows furlough furlong furtive

32. carnage cardiac carbuncle carnivorous cartomancy

33. candidate canvasser canticle cantankerous cantaloup

34. capricious capacity capitation captivate capital

35. endowment endorse endermic endive endocardium

3

WHAT DOES IT MEAN ?

1.

	WORD	*ORIGINAL MEANING*	*LATER MEANINGS*
(*a*)	cash	a box in which money was kept	1. contents of the box 2. ready money
(*b*)	conceit	idea, thought	1. a far-fetched idea, image 2. vanity, pride
(*c*)	delicate	delightful, voluptuous	1. dainty, fine of texture 2. liable to illness
(*d*)	imp	offspring, child	1. mischievous child 2. little devil
(*e*)	nice	tender, delicate	1. precise, fastidious 2. agreeable

2. (*a*) *quick* – original meaning, *alive*; later, *swift*
   (*b*) *silly* – original meaning, *innocent*, *blessed*; later *foolish*
   (*c*) *humour* – original meaning, *fluid* (in the body); later, *mood, state of mind*

3. (*a*) *chamberlain* – originally, a *servant*
   (*b*) *knight* – originally, a *page*, *boy-servant*
   (*c*) *minister* – originally, a *servant*

4. (*a*) *caitiff* – 1. a captive 2. cowardly, despicable person
   (*b*) *knave* – 1. boy 2. rogue
   (*c*) *idiot* – 1. private person, 'layman' 2. fool, imbecile
   (*d*) *libertine* – 1. person set free 2. licentious, dissolute man

5. One of the original body fluids or *humours* was *melancholy*, or black bile, believed to be the cause of depression and sadness.

6. (*a*) MOIETY (*b*) VULGAR (*c*) GENEROUS (*d*) UNCOUTH (*e*) SHREWD

7. (*a*) zest (*b*) pagan (*c*) triumph

8. (*a*) *brave* – originally, finely dressed, worthy of admiration
(*b*) *fond* – originally, foolishly credulous, doting
(*c*) *sad* – sedate or serious

9. anent – concerning
enow – enough
naught – nothing
perchance – perhaps
howbeit – nevertheless
burthen – burden, load
forbears – ancestors
albeit – though
welkin – sky
methought – it seemed to me

10. (*a*) *artful* – originally, *skilful*
crafty – skilful in a trade or art. The later meaning of cunning or deceitful probably represented jealousy or suspicion on the part of the less skilful
(*a*) *erring* – original meaning, *wandering*
vagabond – a wanderer, often (no doubt) discovered to be a rascal; hence the transference of the idea of moral wandering.

11. (*a*) EXTRAVAGANT
(*b*) CYNOSURE
(*c*) FULMINATE
(*d*) ECCENTRIC
(*e*) OFFICIOUS

12. (*a*) allay, alloy (*b*) convey, convoy
(*c*) factitious, fictitious (*d*) reverend, reverent
(*e*) spacious, specious

13. (a) auger, augur (*b*) censer, censor
(*c*) ingenious, ingenuous (*d*) mendacity, mendicity
(*e*) cession, session

14. (*a*) ascent, assent (*b*) complement, compliment
(*c*) levity, lenity (*d*) stationary, stationery
(*e*) vacation, vocation

15. (*a*) astronomy – astrology (*b*) bridal – bridle
(*c*) formerly – formally (*d*) monitory – monetary
(*e*) cymbal – symbol

16. (*a*) anomalous – anonymous (*b*) descent – dissent
(*c*) epitome – epitaph (*d*) junction – juncture
(*e*) momentous – momentary

17. (*a*) marshal (*b*) principal (c) tycoon

(*a*) martial=warlike (*b*) principle=rule, law
(c) typhoon=hurricane

18. (*a*) alternative (*b*) analyst (*c*) ascetic
(*d*) apprised (*e*) apostle

19. (*a*) congenital (*b*) corporal (*c*) continual
(*d*) credible (*e*) courtesy

20. (*a*) deficient (*b*) definitive (*c*) disposition
(*d*) deprecate (*e*) deference

21. (*a*) efficient (*b*) elementary (*c*) epigram
(*d*) erratic (*e*) expedient

22. (*a*) fluent (*b*) fractious (*c*) fallible
(*d*) felicity (*e*) floral

23. (*a*) imaginary (*b*) imperial (*c*) indigent
(*d*) inflammatory (*e*) innocuous

24. (*a*) judicial (*b*) jurisdiction (*c*) liniment
(*d*) licentious (*e*) liquidate

25. (*a*) meditate (*b*) meretricious (*c*) notorious
(*d*) ordnance (*e*) observation

26. (*a*) perspicacity (*b*) plaintive (*c*) practicable
(*d*) presumptive (*e*) punctilious

27. (*a*) recourse (*b*) refectory (*c*) relegate
(*d*) repertoire (*e*) revelation

28. (*a*) sanguine (*b*) sensitive (*c*) sociable
(*d*) stimulant (*e*) supercilious

29. (*a*) temperate (*b*) testament (*c*) topical
(*d*) transitory (*e*) turbid

30. (*a*) ulterior (*b*) urbane (*c*) verbose
(*d*) voluble (*e*) warrant

31. (*a*) *assure* – to make safe, certain, tell confidently
ensure – to secure against risks, make certain a thing shall happen
insure – to secure payment of money in event of loss or damage

(*b*) *credence* – belief
credentials – letters of introduction, qualifications
credit – trust, belief, acknowledgement of merit

(*c*) *euphemism* – mild expression substituted for harsh one
euphony – pleasing sound
euphuism – affected or high-flown style of writing (as in Lyly's *Euphues*, 1580)

(*d*) *primal* – fundamental, primeval, primitive
primary – original, earliest
primitive – ancient, early, old-fashioned

(*e*) *respective* – individual, proper to each in turn, comparative
respectable – worthy of respect, of some importance, fairly good
respectful – showing respect or deference

32. (*a*) *artist* – person practising one of the arts, esp. painting
artiste – a professional singer, dancer, etc.

(*b*) *ay* – yes, an affirmative answer
aye – ever, always

(*c*) *cord* – string or thin rope
chord – 1. combination of simultaneous notes
2. string of musical instrument

(*d*) *by* – near or beside, in company of (prep. and adverb)
bye – subordinate, secondary (e.g. run in cricket)

(*e*) *forgo* – to go without, abstain from, relinquish
forego – to go before, precede

(*f*) *human* – belonging to or having qualities of man
humane – kindly, benevolent

(*g*) *loose* – adj. freed from restraint; verb. set free
loosen – relax, make less tight or firm

(*h*) *moral* – relating to regulation of conduct, difference between right and wrong
morale – a moral state or condition, especially in regard to a high standard of discipline

(*i*) *wake* – 1. verb. to rouse from sleep; 2. kind of festival; 3. smooth water path left behind a ship
awake – rouse(d) from sleep, vigilant

(*j*) *wave* – 1. noun. swell of water; 2 verb. to vibrate, make gesture of the hand
waive – to relinquish, give up, forgo

33. (*a*) *adverse* – contrary, opposite, hostile
averse – unwilling, disinclined, opposed to

(*b*) *distinct* – separate, not identical, clear
distinctive – characteristic, special, unmistakable

(*c*) *economic* – belonging to economics, maintained for profit
economical – thrifty, not wasteful

(*d*) *historic* – of importance in history. (N.B. Certain grammatical tenses are called '*historic*')
historical – of the past, not legendary

(*e*) *precipitate* – verb. to fling, hurl, hasten; adjective. hasty, hurried
precipitous – steep, like a precipice

(*f*) *advice* – noun. information or information offered
advise – verb. to offer advice or counsel; announce

(*g*) *childish* – like a child, puerile (in adults)
childlike – having the qualities of a child (e.g. curiosity)

(*h*) *effectual* – valid, fulfilling its purpose
effective – impressive, striking

(*i*) *indict* – accuse, lay a charge against
indite – to write, compose in words

(*j*) *venal* – able to be bought, prepared to sacrifice principles for profit
venial – excusable, pardonable (of sin or offence)

34. (*a*) *affect* – to move, touch, produce effect; assume, pretend
effect – to accomplish, bring about result; n. result, consequence

(*b*) *councillor* – member of a council
counsellor – adviser

(*c*) *delusion* – false impression or opinion
illusion – deception (especially of the senses)

(*d*) *elicit* – draw out, evoke, educe
illicit – unlawful, forbidden

(e) *reversal* – a turning to opposite nature or effect
reversion – a return to previous state or habit

(*f*) *decided* – resolved, settled, definite
decisive – conclusive

(*g*) *exceeding* – surpassing, going beyond, greater than
excessive – exceeding proper amount

(*h*) *lifelong* – lasting for a lifetime
livelong – whole length of day or period

(*i*) *purport* – sense or meaning
purpose – object

(*j*) *virtual* – in effect but not in form
virtuous – possessing moral goodness, chaste

35. *aggravate* – to intensify, increase gravity of; liable to be used in sense of to annoy or exasperate
awfully – inspiring awe; used carelessly for '*notable, very*', to emphasise (e.g. awfully good)
between – often used instead of the correct preposition 'among' for more than two persons or things
chronic – used in slang for 'bad' or 'severe'. Meaning, when applied to diseases, is 'lingering', opposite of 'acute'
due – used incorrectly for 'owing' (e.g. He was absent due to a bereavement.)
hectic – refers to kind of feverish flush in illness; misapplied to other kinds of excitement (e.g. a hectic holiday)

literally – meaning 'exact to the letter', often misused as an intensive (e.g. I was literally frozen)
mutual – reciprocal; used wrongly instead of 'common' (as in the Dickens' title, *Our Mutual Friend*)
nice – a 'lazy' word used for every kind of pleasant thing or experience. Correctly, 'precise', etc.
transpire – used loosely for 'occur' or 'happen'; proper meaning, 'to come to light', 'become known'

36. ataraxy – stoical indifference
bort – diamond fragments made in cutting
compotation – tippling, drinking together
dyspnoea – difficult breathing
gunny – coarse sacking
guttate – speckled
kloof – deep narrow valley in South Africa
lucifugous – shunning daylight
merganser – diving fish-eating duck
ochlocracy – mob rule

37. eupeptic – having good digestion
fatidical – gifted with prophetic power
glabrous – smooth-skinned, free from hair
hepatic – good for the liver
hircine – goat-like
intagliated – carved on the surface
malm – soft chalky rock
nenuphar – a water lily
revetment – a retaining-wall
torticollis – stiff neck

38. *murder* – term used (under British law) for killing which is intended and planned
manslaughter – term used for killing which is not planned, though possibly intended
homicide – includes both *murder* and *manslaughter* (in the U.S.A., the Homicide Squad deals with all kinds of killing)

39. (*a*) *infer* – to derive or deduce from given facts or ideas
    imply – to mean, signify, hint at
    (*b*) *inherent* – intrinsic, essential, indwelling
    innate – inborn, natural

40. (*a*) *prostrate* – lying face downwards
    supine – lying face upwards, on one's back
    (The worshipper in the hymn would obviously be risking a cricked neck)
    (*b*) *agnostic* – one who says it is impossible to prove the existence of God
    atheist – one who denies the existence of God

4

HOW DO YOU SPELL IT ?

1. isle fare mews poll | brayed grease mien wrest | kerb hart neigh sighed | deign hymn hour tracked | draft loch plumb throne

1. isle	brayed	kerb	deign	draft
fare	grease	hart	hymn	loch
mews	mien	neigh	hour	plumb
poll	wrest	sighed	tracked	throne

2. adze	broach	cruise	due	fête
gild	haul	colonel	leak	manor
pier	choir	route	shear	trait
yews, ewes	veil	waste	yolk	quay

3. (*a*) heir – air – ere
(*b*) cite – sight – site
(*c*) coarse – corse – course
(*d*) fane – feign – fain
(*e*) hue – Hugh – hew
(*f*) meet – meat – mete
(*g*) pear – pair – pare
(*h*) write – right – wright
(*i*) praise – prays – preys
(*j*) vane – vain – vein

4. awful	desiccated	library	medicine
obbligato	persuade	radiance	separate
stupefy	teetotaller		

5. 10 mistakes. The correct spellings are:

physicist	successful	quarrelling	Piccadilly
piccalilli	connoisseur	embarrass	dissatisfied
accessibility	paralleled		

6. (*a*) apophthegm (*b*) fidgety (*c*) languorous
(*d*) propaganda (*e*) inoculate (*f*) variegated
(*g*) transcendent (*h*) mischievous (*i*) resuscitate
(*j*) honorary

7. These 9 words were incorrectly spelt:

diarrhoea	diphtheria	erysipelas	dyspepsia
jaundice	pneumonia	meningitis	quinsy
tonsillitis			

8. No. Two words, *thunderous* and *disastrous* were wrongly spelt. One word, *dext*(*e*)*rous*, may be spelt in two ways.

9.

biassed	burned	cypher	connexion	inquiry
focusing	gypsy	hiccough	gaol	pygmy

10.

antennae	bacilli	dogmas	formulas(or–ae)	grotto(e)s	
octopuses	neuroses	geniuses, genii	salvoes	trousseaux	

11. 3 words incorrectly spelt. Correct spellings: frieze, seize, mien

12. Both forms allowed. Many good writers retain the 'e', though omission of this letter is generally favoured

13. Errors frequently made:

areoplane	buisness	ashphalt	guage	fuschia
gramaphone	parliment	goverment	sincerly	villian

14. a*l*moner bom*b*er condi*g*n de*b*tor *g*nome
*p*sychology *m*nemonic *p*tarmigan *h*eirloom *k*nout

15. Recommended spellings: (*a*) coconut – but cokernut in commercial usage (*b*) eyrie – but all four forms allowed (*c*) doily (*d*) chute (*e*) melodeon – but -dion, and -dium allowed

16. 6 names incorrectly spelt. Corrected spellings:
accordion cello clarinet saxophone
ukelele (or ukulele) violin

17. aching argument annulment
beautify humorous piteous
reliable transferring usable
wasteful

18. 5 names incorrectly spelt. Corrected spellings:
Buddha Caesar Galileo Mendelssohn Tchaikovsky

19. fourth ninth twelfth eighteenth twenty-first
thirtieth forty-fourth fifty-eighth sixty-seventh
ninety-ninth

20. archery boundary customary directory elementary
factory granary honorary inventory jewellery

21. armadillo buffalo cheetah dromedary giraffe
hippopotamus hyena jackal kangaroo opossum
rhinoceros

22. clarion bludgeon guardian bunion galleon
surgeon custodian musician carrion oblivion

23.

anxiety	brutality	piety	agility	nicety
activity	sobriety	docility	gaiety	extremity

24.

coast	hoes	poultry	moan	mould
throes, throws	knows	oath	own	foes

25.

article	bicycle	icicle	canticle	medical
vehicle	tragical	practical	particle	vertical

26.

anaesthetic	casualty	disease	chloroform
massage	ointment	medicine	physician
diagnosis	sterilise		

27.

accustom	fulcrum	laburnum	rostrum	phantom
decorum	emporium	idiom	ransom	tedium

28. baronet, excellency, governor, consul, licentiate, superintendent were misspelt

29.

agency	argosy	fluency	pleurisy	clemency
courtesy	heresy	leprosy	tenancy	currency

30.

brigantine	canteen	crinoline	gelatine	convene
quarantine	supervene	contravene	tambourine	libertine

31.

athlete	conceit	forfeit	(1) discreet (2) discrete	entreat
replete	obsolete	secrete	complete	effete

32. 6 words correctly spelt: aria, fugue, rallentando, intermezzo, polonaise, staccato

5

HOW DO YOU SAY IT ?

1. a-*dew*' ab*doh*'men *ee*'-pok – roe-*bust*' *vahz*

2. a-*doh*'-bi (3 syllables) *bourzh*'-wah (2) *seer*'-ment (2) *clere*'-story (3) eks-*tem*'-por-i (4) eks-*tror*'-din-ar-i (5) fewr-*or*'-i (3) *in*'-ter-est-ing (4) *lin*'-i-ej (3) *med*'-s'n (2)

3. *kon*'-dit (silent 'u') feef ('o') *jep*'-ar-di ('o') *mor*'-gij (silent 't') *pos*'-tew-mus ('h', 'o') rag-*oo*' ('t') *rahz*'-ber-i ('p') *ron*'-day-voo ('z', 's') ser-*ahl*'-yo ('g') *sut*'l (b')

4. | | | | | |
|---|---|---|---|---|
| *ee*'-on | *ay*'-gew | bawk | sha-*green*'
sha-*grin*' | *eg*'-o |
| fa-*sahd*' | *fra*'-cah | *he*'-lot | in-*dyt*' | la-*pel*' |
| meen | mor-*ahl*' | nayv
nah-*eev*' | *or*'-ji | *pos*'-si |
| skayn | shee
skee | siv | skon
skohn | tryst |

5. *Chek*'-ov *Dew*'-mah *Geu*'-te *Vahg*'-ner Mak-i-a-*vel*'-i *Mote*'-zart *Peeps* Pik-*aht*'-so *Hie*-d'n *Zayv*'-iei

6. *al*'-mon-er *an*'-ti-kwar-i *ar*'-ki-tekt ar-*tif*'-i-ser
ahmn'-er
ar-*teest*' *shoh*'-fur ky-*rop*'-o-dist kon-*tro*'ler
kom-an-*dant*' eks-*ek*'-u-tor fin-*an*'-si-er *glay*'-zher
jy-ne-*kol*'-o-jist ly-*brayr*'-i-an mass-*erz*'
gy-ne-*kol*'-o-jist
met-*tal*'-ur-jist *os*'-ler *sem*'-stress
stee've-dor *vitl*'-er

7. *ar*'-ris-toh-krat *ka*'-pit-al-ist chi-cher-*roh*'-nay
kon-i-*ser*' dil-et-*an*'-ti fa-*keer*' *may*'-tri-ark
play'-j(i)ar-ist *prem*'-i-er viz-*eer*'

8. *day*'-li-ah a*nem*'-e-ni *klem*'-a-tis *sik*'-la-men
ay'-dl-vys esh-*sholt*'-si-a *hie*'-a-sinth *ma*'-ri-gold
pent-*stem*'-on *vie*'-o-la

9. *ee*'-gret flam-*in*'-go *gil*'-i-mot *hal*'-si-on *os*'pray
pluv'-er *tar*'-mi-gan *thro*'sl *whee*'-teer *wi*'jn

10. ka-*mel*'-o-pard koy-*oh*'-ti new ig-*wah*'-na *eye*'-beks
kam-el-o-pard
lem'-ewr o-*kah*'-pi o-*poss*'-m *pol*'fri *zee*'-bra
lee'-mewr

11. a-poj-a-*too*'-ra *ah*'-ri-a ar-*pej*'-yoh *tshel*'-lo
des'kant fan-ta-*zee*'-a shay-*nah*'-ri-o *skert*'-so
fan-*tah*'-zi-a se-*neh*'-ri-o
fan-*tay*'-zi-a
ve-*oh*'-la son-*ah*'-ta

12. (*a*) al-*bee*'-noh *al*'-i-by a-*mee*'-ba ba-*sill*'-us
kam-pan-*eel*'-i *kly*'-entel day-*boo*' fa-*sahd*'
fun'-ji *gay*'-la *neg*'-li-zhay
fun'gi *gah*'-la
non'-par-el sub-*pee*'-na

(b)	ay-pry-*oh*’-ry	bass-re-*leef*’	*boh*-na *fy*’-de
	shay *dervr*’	koo day-*tah*’	kool de *sak*’
	fo-*pah*’	pry-mah *fay*’-shi-ee	ray-son *daytr*’
	sahn-*frwah*’	sy-ni *dy*’-ee	sot-oh *voh*’-chay
	tah-bl-*doht*’	tayt-a-*tayt*’	toot on-*sawm*’-bl

13.	*ap*’-lik-a-bl	klan-*des*’-tin	kom-*mew*’-nal	*kom*’-par-abl
	kon’-ver-sant	*dek*’-a-dent	dek-*ohr*’-us	*des*’-pik-abl
	dis’-ip-lin-a-ri	*dis*’-pew-tabl	dok-*try*’-nal	
			dok’-tri-nal	
	eks’-kwi-zit	*for*’-mid-abl	*hos*’-pit-abl	
	il-*lus*’-tra-tiv	*im*’-pi-us	ir-re-*mee*’-di-abl	
	ir-*rep*’-ar-abl	*lam*’-en-tabl	*law*’-da-tori	

14.	man-*ny*’-ak-al	*mis*’-chiv-us	*moh*’-ment-ar-i
	non’-sha-lant		
	new-miz-*mat*’-ik	*ob*’-dew-rayt	ob-*li*’-ga-to-ri
		ob-*dew*’-rayt	*ob*’-lig-a-to-ri
	or-tho-*pee*’-dik	*pref*’-er-abl	*pos*’-tew-mus
	ref’-ew-tabl	re-*mee*’-di-abl	*sal*’-yew-tar-i
	see’-kret-iv	*sedn*’-tar-i	son-*ohr*’-us
	sik-*ree*-tiv		*son*’-ohr-us
	tem’-por-ari	yew-*bik*’-wi-tus	*vee*’-e-ment
	vie’-bra-tor-i		

15.	a-*koo*’-stiks	al-*bew*’-men	a-*men*’-ity
	as’-pir-ant	*awk*’-shun	bra-*vah*’-doh
	as-*pyr*’-ant		
	sen-*tee*’-nar-i	*chas*’-tiz-ment	*kyar*’-os-*koor*’-oh
	kon’-tro-ver-si	*kurt*’-es-i	*sin*’-o-shoor
	din’-ast	*en*’-i-ma	*es*’-pi-on-ij
			es-pi-on-*ahzh*

16.		
for’-red	gool	*glas’*-i-er
gyr’-o-skope	*hay’*-rem har-*eem’*	*im’*-be-seel
in’-ven-tor-i	*lab’*-or-a-tor-i lab-*or’*-at-or-i	*lah’*-ther
lon-*jev’*-iti	mak-in-*ay’*-shun	*mok’*-as-in
pan-e-*jyr’*-ic	plahk	*pres’*-sed-ens pri-*seed’*-ens

17.			
proh’-file *proh’*-feel	*prot’*-ay-zhay	*toh’*-mayn	*kwon’*-dar-i
kwesti-on-*air’*	re-*kog’*-niz-ans	*res’*-pit	root
sat-*ty’*-i-ti	*shed’*-ewl	*sy’*-ne-kewr	*soh’*-bri-kay
sol’-i-sism	*tee’*-nit *ten’*-it	tor-*nay’*-doh	*yew’*-rin-al
va-*gayr’*-i *va’*-gayr-i	*ver’*-di-gris	*vit’*-a-min *vie’*-ta-min	*ways’*-koht *wes’*-kut

18.	
(*a*) *at’*-trib-ute	(*b*) at-*trib’*-ute
(*a*) *buff’*-et	(*b*) *boo’*-fay
(*a*) kom-*pakt’*	(*b*) *kom’*-pakt
(*a*) con-*flict’*	(*b*) *con’*-flict
(*a*) *kon’*-sort	(*b*) kon-*sort’*
(*a*) *kon’*-sum-mayt	(*b*) kun-*sum’*-mayt
(*a*) *kon’*vers	(*b*) kon-*vers’*
(*a*) kon-*vikt’*	(*b*) *kon’*-vikt
(*a*) de-*fyl’*	(*b*) *dee’*-fyl
(*a*) *dy’*-jest	(*b*) di-*jest’*

19.	
(*a*) dis-*kownt’*	(*b*) *dis’*kownt
(*a*) fort	(*b*) *for’*-tay
(*a*) fre-*kwent’*	(*b*) *free’*-kwent
(*a*) *gal’*-ant	(*b*) gal-*lant’*
(*a*) *in’*-sens	(*b*) in-*sens’*
(*a*) in-*val’*-id	(*b*) *in’*-val-eed
(*a*) ob-*jekt’*	(*b*) *ob’*-jekt
(*a*) *proj’*-ekt	(*b*) proh-*jekt’*
(*a*) sahv	(*b*) salv
(*a*) sluff	(*b*) slou

20. In the following words, 'al-' is pronounced *awl-*:
albeit alderman almanac almost alter altercate alternate

In these words it is pronounced *al-*:
albino albumen alchemy alcove almoner alphabet altitude altruism

21. If you come from the North Country or the Midlands and use the short or flat 'a' and 'o' in all these words (as you are entitled to do), you have no problems. The pitfalls are for those who affect (often illogically) the long vowel sounds of the South. The following recommendations are supported by the *Concise Oxford Dictionary, Modern English Usage*, and other authorities:

loss (pronounce lawss or loss) *pass* (pahss or pass)
bath (bahth or bath *class* (class) *coffee* (coff- not cawf-)
cross (cross or crawss) *dog* (not dawg) *glass* (glass)
grass (grass) *lass* (not lahss) *laugh* (lahf or laff)
mass (mass) *off* (off or awf) *often* (aw'fn or off'n)
path (pahth or path) *revolve* (not-vawlv) *soft* (soft, sawft)

Inconsistencies abound. You may say *pahss* for 'pass', but apparently not *mahss* for 'mass' or *lahss* for 'lass', and certainly not *ahss* for 'ass'. TV advertisements have made us familiar with the soap with the bountiful *lah'dher*, but *Modern English Usage* notes that the *Oxford English Dictionary* gives only *lather*, suggesting that this word 'does not belong to the class in which *ah* and ā are merely southern or northern variants'.

6

HOW'S YOUR GRAMMAR?

1. Sentence (*a*) to be preferred. Verb in singular number required after distributive adjective '*every*'.

2. Sentence (*b*). Subject '*None*' (– 'not one') is singular and requires verb in singular number, though usage often allows the plural.

3. Sentence (*a*). The composite subject (two nouns in singular number joined together by *either-or* or *neither-nor* requires singular verb.

4. Sentence (*a*). Singular verb required by composite subject (singular nouns joined by 'as well as').

5. Sentence (*b*). The demonstratives '*this*', '*those*', etc. should agree in number with the nouns they qualify

6. Sentence (*a*). Verb in adjectival clause has plural subject 'who', qualifying 'girls'.

7. Sentence (*b*). '*Each other*' is used of two persons or things, but these 'reciprocal pronouns' are often confused.

8. Sentence (*b*). It is not suggested that the children are smaller than they used to be. '*Less*', the comparative of '*little*', refers not to number but to size.

9. Sentence (*b*).The preposition 'between' should be followed by a 'dual' noun – representing two persons or things.

10. Sentence (*a*). Distributive pronoun '*either*' should be followed by singular verb.

11. Sentence (*b*). The preposition '*between*' governs the objective form of the pronoun.

12. Sentence (*a*). As the Chairman is not the same person as the Vice-Chairman, it is necessary to repeat the definite article.

13. Sentence (*b*). The possessive case should be used for a pronoun followed by a gerund.

14. Sentence (*a*). Nominative case of pronoun required as subject of verb '*will be*'.

15. Sentence (*b*). After verb '*to be*', nominative case of pronoun is required.

16. Sentence (*b*). Obviously the dog was not accompanying himself on the guitar. The 'unrelated participle' '*Playing*' agrees in syntax with 'dog', but in sense with 'he' understood. It should be noted that a participle qualifies the subject of the nearest finite verb.

17. Sentence (*a*). Confusion of past participle '*written*' with past tense '*wrote*'.

18. Sentence (*b*). The 'Split Infinitive' – undesirable because inelegant, though defended by some when (occasionally) there is risk of ambiguity.

19. Sentence (*a*). Inelegant form of verb used in (*b*), though the expression (*didn't use*) is frequently used by inelegant speakers. The auxiliary verb is not required here.

20. Sentence (*b*). Subjunctive mood required ('*were*') when conjunction '*If*' introduces a supposition.

21. Sentence (*b*). Sentence (*a*) is one example of the incorrect use of ellipsis. Verb should not be omitted after subject unless same part of verb is understood.

22. Sentence (*a*). Another example of faulty ellipsis. Logically, the conjunction '*than*' cannot serve for both constructions.

23. Sentence (*b*). The indefinite pronoun '*one*' should be followed by '*one's*', also indefinite, not by the personal pronoun '*his*'.

24. Sentence (*a*). The word '*like*' (an adjective or an adverb) should not be used as a conjunction.

25. Sentence (*b*). The word '*without*' is a preposition, not a conjunction.

26. Sentence (*b*). The adverb of emphasis '*only*' should be placed near the word it modifies.

27. Sentence (*b*). The two verbs, '*I will*' (indicating determination) and '*I shall*' (futurity), are often confused, sometimes with amusing results. (e.g. the well-known sentence: 'I *will* drown and nobody *shall* save me!' – attributed to a foreign student, out of his depth in both the river and his English grammar.)

28. Sentence (*b*). It is not considered 'good English' to qualify the absolute.

29. Sentence (*a*). In (*b*) the correlative conjunction is misplaced. This should immediately precede the words it connects.

30. Sentence (*b*). The word '*as*' should not be used as a relative pronoun.

31. Sentence (*b*). The word '*Due*', which is adjectival in function, should be logically related to its noun or pronoun.

32. Sentence (*a*). As cause is indicated in '*reason*', sentence (*b*) is an example of tautology; but 'the reason is because . . .' is unfortunately so common that it has almost acquired the sanction of usage.

33. Sentence (*b*). In (*a*), the adverbs '*there*' and '*here*' are wrongly used as adjectives.

34. Sentence (*b*). In (*a*) the word '*don't*', which is the contraction of '*do not*', does not agree with '*he*'.

35. Sentence (*a*). In (*b*), 'what' is wrongly used as a relative pronoun. Pronoun 'him' and verb 'done' incorrect.

36. Sentence (*b*). 'Try and-' is incorrect as a substitute for 'try to-', but the expression is common usage and is defended by some grammarians as an example of hendiadys (the expression of a compound notion by treating its two constituent parts as though they were independent).

37. Sentence (*b*). The use of 'a lot of' for 'many' is also accepted usage, but Eric Partridge, in *Usage and Abusage*, reminds us that it is not 'Standard English' and its use 'where any refinement or elevation of language is required is impossible'.

38. Sentence (*a*). It is incorrect to make '*between*' govern a singular noun, as in sentence (*b*).

39. Sentence (*b*). Confusion of two verbs results in an impropriety frequently encountered and generally condoned. It should be remembered, however, that '*can*' refers to capacity or ability to do something; '*may*' to permission or sanction.

40. Sentence (*b*). In (*a*) the Present Infinitive, not the Perfect Infinitive, is required, to avoid a faulty sequence.

7

WHERE DO WE STOP ?

1. (*a*) colon (:) (*b*) full stop (.)
   (*c*) comma (,) (*d*) exclamation mark (!)
   (*e*) apostrophe (') (*f*) hyphen (by-law)
   (*g*) inverted commas ("...") or quotation marks (*h*) dash (—)
   (*i*) inverted commas ('...') (*j*) question mark (?)

2. (*a*) 'Why?' did you say? I told you why. I thought I had made myself clear. To all, I mean, who were paying attention. (4 sentences)

   (*b*) The old-fashioned remedy of counting 'A flock of sheep that leisurely pass by', the poet Wordsworth included in his '*Sonnet to Sleep*' as one of the ways in which he had tried to cure his insomnia. (1 sentence)

   (*c*) He tried to run faster, but couldn't do it. On the fresh rise he nearly tripped and fell, but kept up. Cresting the hump of the field, he could see a tall screen of poplars, and some willows in the fold below, and forced himself, limping, down to them. At the bottom was a stream. (4 sentences)

3. (*a*) He dressed in a pale blue shirt, knitted black tie, and a grey suit. He added a topcoat; the day showed every promise of sunshine, but there was a chill wind.

(*b*) 'You are not concentrating, Jones,' Butcher said. 'You must hit with your mind as well as your muscles.'

(*c*) 'Hum!' mused the inspector, stroking his chin. 'By the way,' he continued, 'I wonder whether life is extinct?'

(*d*) 'Why?' he asked innocently. 'The Black Knight – don't you trust him?'

(*e*) 'We – er – you – er – that is —' He tried again, taking another step forward.

4. (*a*) My gardener – we call him 'Bertie' and his official designation is Albert Edward O'Shaughnessy – was, as had been anticipated, conspicuous by his absence.

(*b*) Through a skin-diving mask or glass-bottomed boat you look into a world of almost unbelievable beauty – castle-like coral formations, precipices jewelled with sea fans and hung with exquisitely hued sea plants.

(*c*) Another friend of that period was six-foot Billy, who ate regularly in the café downstairs; a stranded Negro sailor from Troy, Missouri, who had either jumped ship or had lost his way.

(*d*) It was a small, square canvas, labelled: 'Portrait of the Artist, by Himself.'

(*e*) When their general wanted him to have the twenty-four deserters executed as a warning to others, he just went stubborn and said: 'General, there are already too many weeping widows in the United States.'

5. (*a*) Comma after '*money*' inadequate; use semi-colon.

   (*b*) Apostrophe misplaced in *don't*, and omitted in *it's*. Question mark, not exclamation mark to end sentence.

   (*c*) No apostrophe required in '*Theirs*'.

   (*d*) Colon required instead of semi-colon after V.I.P.s.

   (*e*) Colon required after '*her*', comma after '*madam*', and question mark immediately after '*Hotel*', not between the final commas.

6. (*a*) Goalkeeper accused by captain.

   (*b*) Captain accused by goalkeeper.

   (*c*) A third speaker asks whether the captain accused the goalkeeper.

   (*d*) Captain, wonderingly, asks whether goalkeeper at fault.

   (*e*) Goalkeeper, incredulously, asks whether captain at fault.

7. (*a*)

Feb.	P.S.	Mr (or Mr.)	Co.	Bart
Oxon.	Yorks.	MSS.	Cwt.	Dr (or Dr.)

   (*b*) instant – the present month
   i.e. (id est) – that is
   C.O.D. – Cash on Delivery
   Esq. – Esquire
   LL.D. (*Legum Doctor*) – Doctor of Laws
   G.O.M. – Grand Old Man
   Messrs. – Messieurs
   Q.E.D. (*Quod erat Demonstrandum*) – Which was to be proved or demonstrated.
   lbs. – pounds in weight (*libra*)
   viz. (*videlicet*) – namely

8. E.N.S.A. – Entertainments National Services Association
   E.E.C. – European Economic Community; English Electric Company
   U.N.E.S.C.O. – United Nations Educational Scientific and Cultural Organisation
   U.N.O. – United Nations Organisation
   R.A.D.A. – Royal Academy of Dramatic Art
   O.H.M.S. – On Her (or His) Majesty's Service
   P.E.N. – Poets, Playwrights, Editors, Essayists, Novelists
   N.A.A.F.I. – Navy, Army and Air Force Institutes
   N.A.T.O. – North Atlantic Treaty Organisation
   N.A.L.G.O. – National and Local Government Officers

Comma used:

9. (*a*) to separate items in a list
   (*b*) to separate, and give emphasis to a repeated expression
   (*c*) to avoid ambiguity or confusion in expression
   (*d*) to mark off a phrase which may be regarded as an 'aside', commas may be used instead of parenthesis
   (*e*) to mark off an absolute phrase

10 (*a*) Comma required only after 'production', to mark off absolute phrase – not after 'play'
   (*b*) Comma wrongly used instead of semicolon (after 'concert')
   (*c*) Too many commas. Omit comma after 'mill' or, alternatively, omit all commas
   (*d*) Comma required after 'brother' and after 'stars'; semicolon instead of comma after 'things'
   (*e*) Comma required after 'Speech', but not after 'saving'. No comma after 'Chancellor', but one more in £25,850,000.

11. (*a*) Colon after 'said'
    (*b*) Colon after 'shires'
    (*c*) Semicolon after 'velvet'
    (*d*) Colon after 'follows'; semicolon after 'Brown' and 'Smith'
    (*e*) Semicolon after 'human'

12. (*a*) Exclamation mark after 'back'
    (*b*) Question marks after 'free' and 'happy'
    (*c*) Question marks after 'go', 'France', Italy', 'Greece'
    (*d*) Exclamation mark (or full stop) immediately after 'garage'; question mark at end of sentence after inverted commas
    (*e*) Exclamation mark after 'Listen'; question mark after 'locked'

13. Use hyphen in:

ante-room	bomb-proof	by-law
cross-section	guide-book	hall-mark
quarter-day	sitting-room	son-in-law
text-book	title-deeds	

14. Apostrophes in:

(*a*)	Mine's	what's	(N.B. not in *yours*)	
(*b*)	They're	James's	(not in *theirs*)	
(*c*)	You'll	boys'	men's	women's
(*d*)	Can't	it's		
(*e*)	Sam's	sister's (or sisters')	shop's	

15. Porch; hall, 20 ft. long, polished hardwood floor; cloaks cupboard; through lounge with french window to slabbed porch; dining-room/kitchen, 14ft. × 10ft., all modern fittings; luxurious bathroom, including shower unit; tarmacadam forecourt with drive way to brick-built garage. Elegant wrought-iron gate at side with entrance to compact landscaped rear garden.

16. (*a*) 19 . . Ford Capri 1600 GT Automatic. One local owner. Attractively coloured in Royal Purple with black trim; fully equipped with automatic transmission, radio, matching spot and foglights, heated rear window, etc.; taxed Dec. and in first-class condition throughout. Unrepeatable at only £ . . .

(*b*) Radios, washing machines, recorders, we have them all. We can arrange confidential terms, with four years to pay, tube guarantees, speedy installation – in fact, everything a customer wants. Write or phone: Shockproof Electrics.

17. After a pause he said, 'I'll tell you something very strange.'

'Go on,' said Dora.

'There's a huge bell down there in the water.'

'*What*?' said Dora. She half-rose, amazed, scarcely understanding him.

'Yes,' said Toby, pleased with the effect he had produced. 'Isn't it odd? I found it when I was swimming underwater.'

18. Suddenly Mrs. Otis caught sight of a dull red stain on the floor just by the fireplace and, quite unconscious of what it really signified, said to Mrs. Umney, 'I am afraid something has been spilt there.'

'Yes, madam,' replied the old housekeeper in a low voice, 'blood has been spilt on that spot.'

'How horrid!' cried Mrs. Otis. 'I don't at all care for blood-stains in a sitting-room. It must be removed at once.'

The old woman smiled, and answered in the same low, mysterious voice, 'It is the blood of Lady Eleanore de Canterville, who was murdered on that very spot by her own husband, Sir Simon de Canterville, in 1575.'

19. 'Aha! that squeaky board in the butler's pantry!' said Toad. 'Now I understand it!'

'We shall creep out quietly into the butler's pantry - - - ' cried the Mole.

'- - - - - with our pistols and swords and sticks - - - ' shouted the Rat.

'- - - - and rush in upon them,' said the Badger.

'- - - - and whack 'em, and whack 'em, and whack 'em!' cried the Toad in ecstasy, running round and round the room, and jumping over the chairs.

20. *DOYLE*: . . . he's not an Irishman at all.

BROADBENT: Not an Irishman! (He is so amazed by this statement that he straightens himself and brings the stool bolt upright.)

DOYLE: Born in Glasgow. Never was in Ireland in his life. I know all about him.

BROADBENT: But he spoke – he behaved just like an Irishman.

DOYLE: Like an Irishman! Is it possible that you don't know that all this top-o-the-morning and broth-of-a-boy and more-power-to-your-elbow business is as peculiar to England as the Albert Hall concerts of Irish music are? No Irishman ever talks like that in Ireland, or ever did, or ever will.

21. *MARGARET*: Leave her alone. There are some problems you've never had to face.

LAURIE: I should hope so.

(*The telephone in the sitting-room rings. They stare at it.*)

Who the devil's that?

MARGARET: Well, you'd better answer it.

LAURIE: She hasn't told anyone else where we are?

MARGARET: No, No one. She hasn't spoken to anyone. Well, pick it up.

(ANNIE *does so.*)

ANNIE: Room number . . . what's this one? Three two O. Yes . . . . . No . . . Just a moment. It's for Amy.

LAURIE: Amy!
ANNIE: Amy! Phone! It's for you.
(*They wait*. AMY *appears putting on her dressing gown*.)
AMY: For me? How do they know?
LAURIE: I'll tell you.

22. Say first, of God above, or Man below,
What can we reason, but from what we know?
Of Man, what see we, but his station here,
From which to reason, or to which refer?
Thro' worlds unnumber'd tho' the God be known,
'Tis ours to trace him only in our own.

23. 'What did you say?'
'I? Nothing.' 'No? . . .
What was that sound?'
'When?'
'Then.'
'I do not know.'
'Whose eyes were those on us?'
'Where?'
'There.'
'No eyes I saw.'
'Speech, footfall, presence–how cold the night may be!'
'Phantom or fantasy, it's all one to *me*.'

24. And is it true? And is it true,
This most tremendous tale of all,
Seen in a stained-glass window's hue,
A Baby in an ox's stall?
The Maker of the stars and sea
Become a Child on earth for me?

25. The Nobel Prize in Literature is one of the awards stipulated in the will of the late Alfred Nobel, the Swedish scientist who invented dynamite . . . For authors writing in English, it was bestowed upon Rudyard Kipling in 1907, upon W. B. Yeats in 1923, upon George Bernard Shaw in 1925, upon Sinclair Lewis in 1930, upon John Galsworthy in 1932, upon Eugene O'Neill in 1936, upon Pearl Buck in 1938, upon T. S. Eliot in 1948, upon William Faulkner in 1949, upon Bertrand Russell in 1950, upon Sir Winston Churchill in 1953, upon Ernest Hemingway in 1954 and upon John Steinbeck in 1962.

8

WHO WROTE WHAT ?

1. This is Geoffrey Chaucer's explanation of the origin of *The Canterbury Tales*. Twenty-nine pilgrims had met at the Tabard Inn at Southwark to begin a pilgrimage to the tomb of Thomas à Becket at Canterbury. Harry Bailey, the host, suggested that to pass the time pleasantly on their journey each pilgrim should tell four tales, two on the outgoing ride and two on the way back. The teller of the tales which gave most pleasure to the company would be treated to a dinner on their return to the Tabard Inn. Unfortunately, only twenty-five stories were completed by Chaucer, the author of *The Canterbury Tales*.

2. William Langland. His *Piers the Plowman* is a dream-allegory which vividly depicts the wretchedness of peasant life in 14th-century England.

3. Mystery, Miracle and Morality Plays. *Everyman* is the most famous of the Morality plays.

4. Sir Thomas More. *Utopia.*

5. (*a*) Edmund Spenser (1552–1599)
   (*b*) Samuel Johnson (1709–1784)

6. Dr. Faustus, in Christopher Marlowe's play, *The Tragical History of Dr. Faustus.*

7. Brutus was called 'the noblest Roman' by Antony in Shakespeare's *Julius Caesar.*

8. (*a*) *Antony and Cleopatra*
   (*b*) *Timon of Athens*
   (*c*) *Measure for Measure*
   (*d*) *Two Gentlemen of Verona*
   (*e*) *Troilus and Cressida*

9. Francis Bacon. He was a man of great intellect and many talents, but of unscrupulous character and with an inordinate appetite for power and influence. A false friend, he did not hesitate to sacrifice the life of his benefactor, the Earl of Essex.

In 1621, shortly after being made Viscount St. Albans, he was found guilty of accepting bribes (while holding the offices of Solicitor-General and Lord Chancellor) and was condemned to imprisonment in the Tower for life. But the King, James I, 'the wisest fool in Christendom', gave him his freedom the next day and allowed him to leave his heavy fine unpaid.

10. Bacon's passion for scientific knowledge caused him to leave his carriage one wintry day to stuff the carcase of a fowl with snow, as he wished to discover whether this would preserve the flesh. He caught a chill in the bitterly cold weather and died from bronchitis.

11. Richard Lovelace (1618–1658), one of the Cavalier poets, paid for his adherence to the Royalist cause by imprisonment and the confiscation of his estate.

The verse continues:

'Minds innocent and quiet take
  That for an hermitage:
If I have freedom in my love,
  And in my soul am free,
Angels alone, that soar above,
  Enjoy such liberty.'

12. Samson, captured by the Philistines, was so described by John Milton in his poem *Samson Agonistes*.
The novel, *Eyeless in Gaza*, was written by Aldous Huxley.

13. (*a*) John Bunyan (*b*) Christian (*c*) *The Pilgrim's Progress* (*d*) The City of Destruction and the Celestial City

14. Andrew Marvell wrote this of King Charles I at his execution in 1649. The lines appear in Marvell's *Horatian Ode upon Cromwell's Return from Ireland*.

'But with his keener eye
The axe's edge did try.'

15. Samuel Butler (1612–1680), in *Hudibras*.

16. The Diary of Samuel Pepys.

17. John Evelyn (1620–1706), contemporary and friend of Pepys.

18. John Dryden (1631–1700), in his first important poem, *Annus Mirabilis* (or *The Year of Wonders*), wrote of the events of 1666 – the Great Plague, the Great Fire of London, and the naval battles with the Dutch.

19. (*a*) Alexander Pope (1688–1744)
(*b*) *The Rape of the Lock*
(*c*) Belinda

20. *The Drapier Letters*.

21. The question at issue was: Which is the correct end of a boiled egg for the eater to open? In consequence, the Big-Endians and the Little-Endians were always at loggerheads.

22. *The Tatler* was founded in 1709 by Richard Steele, who invited his old school friend Joseph Addison to be a contributor to the paper. Their second journal, *The Spectator*, appeared in March 1711, two months after *The Tatler* ceased publication.

23. Sir Roger de Coverley.

24. (*a*) Daniel Defoe (*b*) *Robinson Crusoe*
(*c*) Alexander Selkirk (*d*) Island of Juan Fernandez

William Cowper (1731–1800) wrote a poem 'On the meditations of Alexander Selkirk' which begins:

'I am monarch of all I survey,
My right there is none to dispute'

25. Alexander Pope (1688–1744) *The Dunciad.*

26. *Rule, Britannia!*

When Britain first at Heaven's command
Arose from out the azure main,
This was the charter of the land,
And guardian angels sung this strain:
'Rule, Britannia! rule the waves!
Britons never will be slaves'.

27. Dr. Johnson. John Milton was paid £5 for *Paradise Lost*, but the Agreement, now in the British Museum, promised an additional £5 after the sale of 1300 copies, and £5 each on the sale of second and third editions.

28. James Thomson (1700–1748), author of *The Seasons* and *The Castle of Indolence*, was the first 18th-century poet to make nature and the countryside his main themes. He wrote in blank verse and the Spenserian stanza, unlike his contemporaries who adhered to the heroic couplet of Pope and his disciples.

29. Samuel Johnson (1709–1784).
   (*a*) As a child he suffered from scrofula, a skin disease known as the 'King's Evil', for which the 'royal touch' was popularly thought to be capable of effecting a cure.
   (*b*) David Garrick
   (*c*) *Rasselas*
   (*d*) He compiled *A Dictionary of the English Language*, which made him famous though not wealthy; it took him eight years to complete, with the aid of paid assistants.

30. Thomas Gray (1716–1771).
The churchyard of Stoke Poges.
Elegy Written in a Country Churchyard.

31. Oliver Goldsmith (1728–1774). *The Vicar of Wakefield.*

32. Thomas Chatterton (1752–1770). *The Rowley Poems* were published as the work of a Bristol poet monk, Thomas Rowley.

33. Robert Burns (1759–1796). The poem, 'Ae Fond Kiss' was his farewell to Nancy:

> 'I'll ne'er blame my partial fancy;
> Naething could resist my Nancy . . .'

34. Samuel Richardson (1689–1761) wrote his novel *Pamela* in the form of fictitious letters through which the heroine tells how her virtue was rewarded.

35. Henry Fielding (1707–1754), author of *Tom Jones Foundling*, was a Bow Street magistrate.

36. *The Castle of Otranto* is the first example in English fiction of the 'Gothic' romantic novel, or novel of terror, an early 'thriller' whose blood-chilling effects were based on the mysteries and superstitions of the distant past.

37. William Cowper (1731–1800) lived with a clergyman and his family at Olney.

38. Richard Brinsley Sheridan (1751–1816). His famous comedies are: *The Rivals* and *The School for Scandal*.

39. The *Lyrical Ballads*, by William Wordsworth (1770–1850) and Samuel Taylor Coleridge (1772–1834), included Wordsworth's *Lines written above Tintern Abbey* and Coleridge's *The Rime of the Ancient Mariner*.

40. 'Bliss was it in that *dawn* to be alive,
But to be *young* was very heaven.'

The reference is to the French Revolution.

41. Wordsworth, Coleridge and Southey. Southey (who was Coleridge's brother-in-law) preceded Wordsworth as Poet Laureate.

42. Lord Byron (1788–1824) wrote this after the enthusiastic reception of *Childe Harold* in 1812.

He died of marsh fever at Missolonghi.

43. John Keats (1795–1821) died of consumption in Italy and was buried in the Protestant Cemetery at Rome.

44. Jane Austen (1775–1817). Her novels include: *Pride and Prejudice, Sense and Sensibility* and *Northanger Abbey.*

45. Percy Bysshe Shelley (1792–1822) was expelled from Oxford for writing a pamphlet entitled *The Necessity of Atheism*. His argument, however, was not against God but against some of the religious beliefs of the day.

He was drowned while sailing with a friend in the Gulf of Spezia. Lord Byron and other friends were present at the cremation of his body on the sea shore.

46. William Wordsworth was speaking of the view, from Westminster Bridge, of the city of London.

47. Lord Byron's comment was on the savage attack made on Keats's poem *Endymion* by a critic of the *Quarterly Review*, which was thought by Shelley and others to have hastened the poet's death.

Byron, who had been attacked by the critics of the *Edinburgh Review* on the publication of his first poems, *Hours of Idleness*, had retaliated with the satirical poem *English Bards and Scotch Reviewers.*

48. Shelley wrote his elegy *Adonais* in praise of Keats.

Perhaps the best known lines in this poem are:

'Life like a dome of many-coloured glass,
Stains the white radiance of Eternity,
Until Death tramples it to fragments.'

Lycidas is John Milton's elegy on the death of his friend, Edward King, drowned while crossing the Irish Sea.

In Memoriam was written by Lord Tennyson after the death in Vienna of his friend, Arthur Henry Hallam, who was engaged to Tennyson's sister.

49. Scott, at the age of 55, was involved in the financial collapse of his printers and publishers. Though not responsible for their failure, he shouldered the burden and resolved to work until the debt of more than one hundred thousand pounds had been paid. With novels, essays and other literary work, he earned nearly forty thousand pounds in two years, but the strain undermined his health and led to paralytic strokes and death at the age of 61.

50. Charles Lamb. His sister Mary, in a sudden frenzy, stabbed and killed her mother with a table knife, and was confined for a period in an asylum.

Charles and Mary Lamb collaborated in *Tales from Shakespeare*, published in 1807. Charles published his book of essays under the title, *Essays of Elia*.

51. Thomas de Quincey (1785–1859), author of *Confessions of an English Opium Eater*, lived for twenty years in the Lake District.

52. Alfred, Lord Tennyson, famous as a poet, turned for a time to the writing of plays, but these had little success on the stage. Several of them, including *Becket* in which Henry Irving had a part, were produced at Drury Lane; *The Promise of May*, which gave rise to the sarcastic comment, was put on at the Globe.

The pen portrait of Tennyson was written by Thomas Carlyle (1795–1881). Tennyson succeeded Wordsworth as Poet Laureate in 1850.

53. Robert Browning (1812–1889).
   (*a*) *Pippa Passes*
   (*b*) Wordsworth (who appeared to have lost his revolutionary fervour)
   (*c*) *How they brought the good news from Ghent to Aix*
   (*d*) Elizabeth Barrett Browning (1806–1861), author of *Sonnets from the Portuguese* and *Aurora Leigh*

54. Dante Gabriel Rossetti (1828–1882).
The Pre-Raphaelite Brotherhood.

55. The Duke of Wellington died in 1852 and Tennyson wrote the Laureate's tribute to him in an *Ode on the Death of Wellington.*

56. *The Rubaiyat of Omar Khayyàm*, by Edward Fitzgerald (1809–1883).

57. (*a*) Charles Dickens (1812–1870) was born at Portsmouth.
   (*b*) His father was imprisoned there for debt.
   (*c*) Charles worked in a blacking factory for six shillings a week.
   (*d*) He mastered the art of shorthand writing.
   (*e*) *The Daily News.*
   (*f*) *Sketches by Boz.*
   (*g*) *The Pickwick Papers.*
   (*h*) (*i*) *A Tale of Two Cities* (*ii*) *Barnaby Rudge.*
   (*i*) He gave readings of his own works.

(*j*) Sarah Gamp (*Martin Chuzzlewit*)
Sam Weller (*Pickwick Papers*)
Mr. Bumble (*Oliver Twist*)
Mr. Micawber (*David Copperfield*)
Sydney Carton (*A Tale of Two Cities*)

58. William Makepeace Thackeray (1811–1863).

Becky Sharp and Rawdon Crawley appear in *Vanity Fair*, Henry Esmond in *Henry Esmond*, a story of the time of Queen Anne, of Marlborough's campaigns and the rising in support of the Old Pretender.

59. Benjamin Disraeli (1804–1881) said this of W. E. Gladstone in a speech at the Riding School, London, in 1878.

Disraeli's novels include: *Sybil*, *Vivien Gray*, *Coningsby* and *Tancred*.

60. George Eliot was the pen-name of Mary Ann Evans (1819–1880).

Mrs. Poyser and Dinah Morris appear in *Adam Bede*. *Romola* deals with the Renaissance; *Silas Marner* tells the miser's story.

61. The Brontë sisters are associated with the Yorkshire moors; their father was incumbent of Haworth Parish Church, near Keighley.

Charlotte Brontë (1816–1855), Emily Brontë 1818–1848), Anne Brontë (1820–1849).

Their brother, Branwell, was believed to have outstanding talents, but was too erratic and unstable to make use of them. He was given to excesses and irrational behaviour.

Charlotte married, and died in childbirth.

Charlotte wrote *Jane Eyre*, *Shirley* and *Villette;* Emily, *Wuthering Heights;* Anne, *Wildfell Hall.*

62. *Westward Ho!* (Kingsley), *Lavengro* (Borrow), *The Cloister and the Hearth* (Reade), *Cranford* (Gaskell), *Barchester Towers* (Trollope), *The Moonstone* (*Collins*).

63. Thomas Hardy (1840–1928) was a native of Dorset and is known as the 'Wessex' novelist. His novels include:

(*a*) *Far from the Madding Crowd.*
(*b*) *Under the Green wood Tree.*
(*c*) *The Return of the Native.*
(*d*) *Tess of the d'Urbervilles.*
(*e*) *Jude the Obscure.*
Jude the Obscure was unfavourably received.
The Dynasts – a chronicle play of the Napoleonic wars.

64. (*a*) Kenneth Grahame – 1908. (*b*) J. M. Barrie–1904.
(*c*) Lewis Carroll – 1865 (*d*) Rudyard Kipling – 1894.
(*e*) Anna Sewell – 1877 (*f*) Thomas Hughes – 1857.
(*g*) Robert Louis Stevenson – 1883.

Black Beauty was written by a woman. *Peter Pan* is a play. *The Wind in the Willows*, *The Jungle Book* and *Black Beauty* are animal stories. Lewis Carroll was the pen name of the Rev. C. L. Dodgson, author of *Alice in Wonderland*.

65. Oscar Wilde (1856–1900). His most successful play, *The Importance of Being Earnest* is a sparkling comedy of manners which has retained its popularity.

The Ballad of Reading Gaol was based on his experiences in prison.

66. John Masefield (1878–1967) told the story of Saul Kane, a reformed drunkard, in *The Everlasting Mercy*.

67. Joseph Conrad (1857–1924).

An Outcast of the Islands
The Arrow of Gold
Under Western Eyes
The Secret Agent
The Nigger of the Narcissus

68. Herbert George Wells (1866–1946).

The First Men in the Moon (1901).
Love and Mr. Lewisham
The Island of Dr. Moreau
The World of William Clissold
The History of Mr. Polly
Mr. Britling Sees it Through

69. Arnold Bennett (1867–1931).
The Five Towns: – Burslem, Hanley, Tunstall, Longton and Stoke

The Grand Babylon Hotel *Riceyman Steps* *Imperial Palace*

70. (*a*) *The Good Companions*
(*b*) *Time and the Conways* and *I have been here before*

71. D. H. Lawrence (1885–1930) was a native of Eastwood near Nottingham. His father was a miner.

(*a*) *The White Peacock* (*b*) *Sons and Lovers*
(*c*) *Lady Chatterley's Lover*

72. *Ulysses*, by James Joyce (1882–1941), is the mental and spiritual odyssey of Leopold Bloom, compressed within twenty-four hours.

Dubliners (short stories), *Portrait of the Artist as a Young Man.*

73. (*a*) John Galsworthy (*b*) W. Somerset Maugham
(*c*) Rudyard Kipling (*d*) E. M. Forster
(*e*) Virginia Woolf (*f*) Evelyn Waugh
(*g*) Aldous Huxley (*h*) Graham Greene
(*i*) George Orwell (*j*) Kingsley Amis

74. Rupert Brooke (1887–1915) was writing of the challenge to youth at the beginning of the First Great War. Obtaining a commission in the Royal Naval Division, he was sent to the Dardanelles and died there of fever.

75. William Butler Yeats (1865–1939), in this short and much-anthologised poem, indulges his 'fancy' for a peaceful rural life on the *Lake Isle of Innisfree*, where he proposes to build a log cabin, keep bees and grow beans . . .

76. *The Waste Land* *A Song for Simeon*
Journey of the Magi *Murder in the Cathedral*

77. (*a*) He was a music critic
(*b*) *John Bull's Other Island*
(*c*) *Pygmalion* (Professor Henry Higgins; Eliza Doolittle; ('Not bloody likely!')
(*d*) *Major Barbara*
(*e*) *Androcles and the Lion*
(*f*) The Nobel Prize for Literature
(*g*) Shaw died in 1950, aged 94.

78. Sir James Barrie ('*Dear Brutus*')
John Drinkwater (*Abraham Lincoln*)
Sean O'Casey (*Juno and the Paycock*)
Noel Coward (*Hay Fever*)

James Bridie (*Tobias and the Angel*)
Samuel Beckett (*Waiting for Godot*)
Dylan Thomas (*Under Milk Wood*)
John Osborne (*Look Back in Anger*)
Harold Pinter (*The Dumb Waiter*)
Robert Bolt (*A Man for All Seasons*)

79. (*a*) W. H. Davies (*b*) William Henry Hudson
(*c*) W. Somerset Maugham (*d*) Samuel Butler
(*e*) Richard Jefferies

80. (*a*) William Golding (*b*) Shelagh Delaney
(*c*) Laurie Lee (*d*) John Braine
(*e*) Alan Sillitoe

9

CAN YOU PLACE THEM ?

1. (*a*) Pearl Buck (*b*) J. B. Priestley
   (*c*) Louisa M. Alcott (*d*) Oliver Goldsmith

2. (*a*) George Crabbe (*b*) Mary Russell Mitford
   (*c*) John Clare (*d*) Oliver Goldsmith

3. (*a*) Edmund Gosse (*b*) D. H. Lawrence
   (*c*) Charles Dickens

4. (*a*) Jane Austen (*b*) Winifred Holtby
   (*c*) Mrs. Henry Wood (*d*) Charles Kingsley

5. (*a*) Kenneth Grahame (*b*) Henry James
   (*c*) Sir James Frazer

6. (*a*) Sir Thomas More (*b*) H. G. Wells
   (*c*) Samuel Butler (*d*) Francis Bacon

7. (*a*) Joseph Conrad (*b*) Kingsley Amis

8. (*a*) Sir Walter Scott (*b*) William Harrison Ainsworth
   (*c*) Arnold Bennett (*d*) Charles Dickens

9. (*a*) George Gissing (*b*) Philip Massinger
(*c*) Robert Louis Stevenson

10. (*a*) Arthur Conan Doyle (*b*) John Galsworthy
(*c*) Jack London (*d*) D. H. Lawrence
(*e*) John Webster (*f*) Wilkie Collins

11. (*a*) Robert Louis Stevenson (*b*) Sir Walter Scott
(*c*) Alexandre Dumas (*d*) Anna Sewell

12. (*a*) Edward Bulwer Lytton (*b*) Edward Bulwer (Lord) Lytton
(*c*) John Fennimore Cooper (*d*) Anthony Trollope

13. (*a*) Christopher Smart (*b*) T. S. Eliot
(*c*) John Dryden (*d*) John Milton

14. (*a*) T. S. Eliot (*b*) John Masefield
(*c*) G. K. Chesterton (*d*) Alan Sillitoe

15. (*a*) E. V. Lucas (*b*) A. A. Milne
(*c*) Compton Mackenzie (*d*) Jeffery Farnol
(*e*) Hilaire Belloc

16. (*a*) Jane Austen (*b*) Samuel Richardson
(*c*) Benjamin Disraeli (*d*) George Du Maurier
(*e*) Hugh Walpole

17. (*a*) Dinah – Alice's cat in *Alice in Wonderland*
(*b*) Flush – Elizabeth Barrett Browning's spaniel
(*c*) Boatswain – Lord Byron's favourite dog

(*d*) Hodge – Dr. Johnson's cat
(*e*) Selima – Horace Walpole's cat

Dinah was the only fictitious pet, but Selima was the the subject of Thomas Gray's poem on a favourite cat drowned in a goldfish bowl.

18. (*a*) Dickens – the others were lords
(*b*) Sir Roger de Coverley – the only fictitious knight in the group.

19. (*a*) *Pickwick Papers* (*b*) *Great Expectations*
(*c*) *A Christmas Carol* (*d*) *The Old Curiosity Shop*
(*e*) *Oliver Twist*

20. Anne Brontë John Galsworthy Rev. C. L. Dodgson Samuel L. Clemens Eric Blair

21. (*a*) colliery district around Eastwood
(*b*) high moors of Devonshire
(*c*) north west of England, Lake District
(*d*) bleak Yorkshire moors around Haworth
(*e*) Wessex

22. Wystan Hugh Auden Gilbert Keith Chesterton
Thomas Stearns Eliot William Wymark Jacobs
John Boynton Priestley Herbert George Wells

23. Addison and Steele Beaumont and Fletcher
Wordsworth and Coleridge Boswell and Johnson
Wyatt and Surrey

24. (*a*) *Guy Mannering*, by Scott – the rest are by Henry James
    (*b*) *Barry Lyndon*, by Thackeray – the rest by Stevenson
    (*c*) *Our Mutual Friend*, by Dickens – the rest by Kingsley

25. (*a*) Mark Twain
    (*b*) D. H. Lawrence
    (*c*) George Borrow
    (*d*) William Cobbett
    (*e*) R. L. Stevenson

OUR PUBLISHING POLICY

HOW WE CHOOSE

Our policy is to consider every deserving manuscript and we can give special editorial help where an author is an authority on his subject but an inexperienced writer. We are rigorously selective in the choice of books we publish. We set the highest standards of editorial quality and accuracy. This means that a *Paperfront* is easy to understand and delightful to read. Where illustrations are necessary to convey points of detail, these are drawn up by a subject specialist artist from our panel.

HOW WE KEEP PRICES LOW

We aim for the big seller. This enables us to order enormous print runs and achieve the lowest price for you. Unfortunately, this means that you will not find in the *Paperfront* list any titles on obscure subjects of minority interest only. These could not be printed in large enough quantities to be sold for the low price at which we offer this series.

We sell almost all our *Paperfronts* at the same unit price. This saves a lot of fiddling about in our clerical departments and helps us to give you world-beating value. Under this system, the longer titles are offered at a price which we believe to be unmatched by any publisher in the world.

OUR DISTRIBUTION SYSTEM

Because of the competitive price, and the rapid turnover, *Paperfronts* are possibly the most profitable line a bookseller can handle. They are stocked by the best bookshops all over the world. It may be that your bookseller has run out of stock of a particular title. If so, he can order more from us at any time—we have a fine reputation for "same day" despatch, and we supply any order, however small (even a single copy), to any bookseller who has an account with us. We prefer you to buy from your bookseller, as this reminds him of the strong underlying public demand for *Paperfronts*. Members of the public who live in remote places, or who are housebound, or whose local bookseller is unco-operative, can order direct from us by post.

FREE

If you would like an up-to-date list of all paperfront titles currently available, send a stamped self-addressed envelope to
ELLIOT RIGHT WAY BOOKS, BRIGHTON RD.,
LOWER KINGSWOOD, SURREY, U.K.